THE CHURCH IN TODAY'S WORLD

WILLIAM POWELL TUCK

Other Books by
William Powell Tuck

THE CHURCH IN TODAY'S WORLD

WILLIAM POWELL TUCK

Parson's Porch
Books
Cleveland, TN

Parson's Porch Books
121 Holly Trail, NW
Cleveland, TN 37311

ISBN: Softcover   978-1-936912-14-8

"To What Church Do You Belong?" was originally published in *Proclaiming the Baptist Vision: The Church,* edited by Walter B. Shurden, published by Smyth & Helwys, Macon, Georgia in 1996. Used by permission of Smyth & Helwys.

This book was printed in the United States of America.

To order additional copies of this book, contact:
Parson's Porch Books
1-423-475-7308
www.parsonsporch.com

For

Ron and Pat Higdon,

Good friends through the years,

Who have known the joys and challenges of
the local church

CONTENTS

PREFACE

The Church has been under attack for centuries, but probably few times in its history have the threats against the church's survival been as subtle and compelling as today. Many are seeking to rewrite the Church's agenda and equate it with their secular needs. Others are espousing a "prosperity gospel" as the menu for the Church today. Others see the Church as merely an extension of their social needs and as a private club to foster their style of life. Others are interested only in the Church growing, no matter how it grows. Numbers are the only important thing to them. Few today realize the radical and revolutionary nature of the Church which our Lord founded and the call he issued for a dynamic allegiance to him and the life-changing commitment he demands of any who would identify with him and his way of discipleship.

Hans Kung has noted that there has been much talk about the Church in the secular world, but he believes that there is no corresponding awareness of what the Church is. "One can only know what the Church should be now," Kung affirms, "if one also knows what the Church was originally. This means knowing what the Church of today should be in the light of the Gospel."[1] This has to be addressed, I believe, by affirming that the Church was founded by Jesus upon the faith and witness of Peter and the other apostles. The Church has even been called "the New Israel," (Mark 14: 58), the New Covenant," (1 Cor. 11: 25), (Heb. 12:24), "the Realm of Redemption," (Eph. 2:20-22), "the Bride of Christ," (Rev. 22: 9), the "body of Christ" (1Cor. 12:27, Rom. 12: 5, Col. 1:8, Eph. 4:12) or the continuing Incarnation of Jesus in the world (Eph. 1: 23), and the "temple of the Holy Spirit (1Cor. 6: 19, Eph. 2: 21). Jesus assured the Church that where two or three gathered in his name, he would be among them (Matt. 18: 20). The writer of the Letter to the Hebrews reminded the early Christian followers "not neglecting to meet together" (Heb.10: 24-25).

In these pages I want to affirm what I believe is the biblical concept of the Church, its nature, function, and purpose in the world. I want to testify to what I believe is right with the Church and seek to examine anew what our Lord intends for his Church to be and do. The Church today is not a perfect instrument in service for Christ and it never has been. Although some have boldly spoken about the demise of the Church, and it is apparent that many mainline churches have drastically declined in attendance and offerings in recent years, there has been, nevertheless, a resurgence of charismatic and conservative churches. The Church always seems to be dying to some, but it never has nor do I believe it will. My now deceased friend, Cecil Sherman, used to say "I have a life-wish for the Church."[2] And so do I. I want the Church to thrive and be productive in its ministry for our Lord. And that is what I am about in this book-- a life-wish for the Church. I have committed my life to being a servant minister in the church. I love the

Church and want to advance its ministry in the world as we seek to follow our Lord. I write these pages as one who is inside the Church and believes in the authentic Church which our Lord founded. In these brief pages I offer some suggestions on how we can strive to be the Church in today's world.

I want to express my appreciation to Carolyn Stice who served for ten years as my secretary and who first helped me to get my thought onto paper. A special word of appreciation is also due Linda McNally who proof-read these pages for me. I send these chapters out with the prayer that it will enable all who read these pages to serve more faithfully in the Church.

[1] Hans Kung, *The Church* (New York: Sheed and Ward, 1967), ix.

[2] Cecil Sherman, *By My Own Reckoning* (Macon, GA: Smyth & Helwys, 2008), 5.

To What Church Do You Belong?
Choosing the Right Church

Driving along the expressway, I noticed a huge billboard that read: *Attend the church of your choice.* What could be more American than that? It is almost as American as apple pie. Attend the church of your choice. America contains more varieties of religious denominations than Baskin Robbins has ice cream. You have lots of choices. Our ancestors wrote an amendment to our constitution that guaranteed that freedom: "Congress shall make no law respecting an establishment of religion, or prohibiting the free exercise thereof." But as good as the phrase, "Attend the church of your choice," is something in it disturbs me. Since it bothers me, it may perturb you. Consider some of the churches available to you in America today.

The Only Understanding of Truth Church

Some persons belong to The Only Understanding of Truth Church. This church claims it has a special handle on truth. Nobody else has the insight into truth. Members of this church narrow all truth to their own focus. They collect religious truth in propositional form, and anyone who would be a part of *the true church* has to ascribe to their set of beliefs. They assert that not only are their beliefs inerrant and infallible, but so is their interpretation of them. They alone have the truth.

Members of this church are rigid, inflexible, unbending, and un- compromising. All other interpretations are elbowed out in the name of their truth claims. After all, if you have truth, as they claim to have it, how dare anyone differ with their view of God or how we are to live as God's children. Persons in this church show no patience with religions such as Hinduism, Buddhism, Confucianism, or Taoism that allow tolerance for the beliefs of others. Their spirit is linked closely with the fundamentalist strains of Islam that react with vindictiveness to destroy any other religious perspective differing from their own. If you do not belong to The Church with the Only Understanding of Truth, then you are an infidel.

This church's heritage reaches back through the centuries and finds its roots in a perversion of ancient Judaism. Israel declared boldly that it was God's only true people. Some among the Jewish people nobly understood this calling in terms of service to the world. But some misunderstood and transformed the calling into an arrogant and privileged status. The latter stressed their chosenness, emphasizing all others' lack of chosenness.

Our Lord encountered members of this church when he came to minister. The scribes and Pharisees belonged to that kind of church and held tenaciously and rigidly to their interpretation of religion. How dare Jesus challenge their interpretation of the truth! They knew they had the only correct knowledge of religious truth, and they helped crucify Jesus because he dared to challenge their understanding of life.

Saul belonged for a while to The Only Understanding of Truth Church. He persecuted the early Christian church and even held the outer garments for the men who stoned Stephen. But when claimed by Christ, Paul immediately disassociated himself from that religious church. Before long, however, he encountered another form of that same kind of church. It stated that unless Christians became Jews (were circumcised), they could not be true Christians. Paul spent his life arguing for a different and more tolerant kind of church.

Down through the centuries, The Only Understanding of Truth Church has sought to dominate and control the beliefs of others. We often think of the members of this church as bigots. Do you know the origin of that word, bigot? It comes from a condensation of "by God!" "By God." these persons assert, "I have got all the truth, and I am going to cram it down your throat, control your thinking, and make everybody else believe just like I do."

The Inquisition sprang from those who belonged to The Only Understanding of Truth Church. When anybody dared differ with established truth, they were put to death. In 1572, Catherine de Medici executed 20,000 French Protestants because they differed with the established church of that day. The pope sent her a letter congratulating her on the Saint Bartholomew's Day massacre. John Wycliffe translated the Scriptures from Latin into English and so outraged the established church that it condemned him to death. While the church condemned him, because of his protection, it could not harm him. After his death, however, the pope had his bones dug up and burned and his ashes cast into a river so he would not have a place of burial.

Do not think, however, that Catholics have a monopoly on intolerance in Christian history. John Calvin, one of the foremost leaders in the Protestant Reformation, executed a Spanish physician, named Servetus, who differed with him on his interpretation of the Trinity. When the Puritans hounded Roger Williams out of Salem Colony in 1636, he promptly founded Providence, Rhode Island, where all persons might have religious freedom.

The Only Understanding of Truth Church is not confined to any one religion or any single expression of Christianity. It cuts across all denominations. Freedom-loving Baptists, of all persons, one might think, would never be members of that church. Two of the foundational concepts in Baptists' beliefs are the priesthood of all believers and religious tolerance. But, not too many generations ago, Crawford Toy and William Whitsitt had to resign their positions at Southern Baptist Theological Seminary because they were considered heretics when they employed critical tools in their understanding of the Bible.

Now today, several generations later, members of The Only Understanding of Truth Church have paraded across the Baptist denominational landscape once again. Lifting up their banners of truth and engaging in theological witch hunts, they have remove professors from colleges and seminaries that differ with those who claim to have the only correct understanding of truth. Members of this distorted church unfortunately see truth as finished. God has spoken; but God doesn't continue to speak. According to their view, God simply cannot be at work within the church bringing individuals new and fresh visions of divine will and ways. Truth for them is finished and regulated.

When I was a pastor in Virginia, I came in from lunch one day and saw two ministers engaged in conversation with my secretary. It was obvious that they were preachers. They were dressed in the uniforms that quickly convey that message, and they spoke with stained-glass voices. I spoke to them as I came in the door, and started to move on past them since I did not recognize them. Suddenly, I realized that they were theologically attacking my secretary. They were seeking to convert her. You need to know that she was a fine Episcopalian. She had been a secretary at the church for years, and I had never tried to proselytize her into the Baptist fold. She attended her own church and worshiped faithfully. So I turned to them and said: "Pardon me, but I don't believe I like the way you are talking to my secretary." They then turned to me and began to attack me. "Do you believe such and such?" I had an appointment in a few minutes, and I said: "Friend, I would love to have time to debate with you about this theological issue, but I do not. I know 'whom I have believed,' and I am very happy in my faith, and I hope you are in yours. God bless you. I have to go and do some other work."

17

Several weeks later one of our church members told me that she went to another city to attend a funeral service. The ministers, in that funeral service of all places, stood before the grieving family and declared: "You wouldn't believe what a preacher up in Harrisonburg told me that he doesn't believe." Then he began to list a long series of things that he said I did not believe. Well, it so happened that I did believe those things he said I denied. But the worst part is that he had never discussed any of those beliefs with me to know whether I believed them or not. If you refused to dialogue with him about his beliefs, he assumed you did not believe as you should. He already had the right belief, and any who did not agree was a heretic. We have too many of these theological witch hunters in Baptist life today who belong to The Only Understanding of Truth Church. They exclude rather than include sisters and brothers of the faith.

In his novel *Julian,* Gore Vidal depicts a scene in the fourth century where the Roman emperor Julian replaced Christianity as the official religion and restored the pagan gods. He considered Christianity dangerous and immoral. One of his aides asked him if he was going to outlaw Christianity as Christianity outlawed the worship of the pagan gods and persecute the Christians as the Christians had persecuted those who worshiped the pagan gods? "No, leave them alone," Julian said in effect. "I think sooner or later the Christians will kill off each other."

What an indictment on the church! We will kill each other off! Did you read the quip by Henlee Barnette? "Have you noticed that when a minister begins to play God, he winds up acting like the devil?" When anybody thinks they have the only truth about God, they are dangerous. Unfortunately, too many people belong to this church.

The Warm Feeling, Friendly, Everybody-Always-Happy, Noncontroversial, Easygoing, Crowd-Pleasing, Entertaining Church

Others hold membership in another church. They belong to The Warm Feeling, Friendly, Everybody-Always-Happy, Noncontroversial, Easygoing, Crowd-Pleasing, Entertaining Church. Its membership is widespread. People join this church basically to get their own individual needs satisfied. It offers them exactly what they want. Whatever they want, the church is obligated to provide it. This church offers programs for every age—children, teenagers, singles, young adults, and older adults. Whatever people desire, it is satisfied by this church. I recently saw a sign which typifies this church: "Come as you are and relax with us." Did Jesus call us to come and relax?

This church never engages in anything controversial. It doesn't want anything to create disturbances or disharmony. Everything is done to make people feel good and be happy. Nothing controversial is ever allowed or mentioned. The pulpit of this church spews simple sermons for satisfied minds. Preached here are pleasing, peaceful platitudes for pious, placid persons. Disturbances, moral or otherwise, are not tolerated.

Worship services are planned primarily for their entertainment value. The more the spectators feel they have been entertained, the more they think they have worshiped. When they leave this church, they want to feel warm and cozy inside. The worship of Almighty God becomes the theological equivalent of a Lawrence Welk *Variety Hour* or *American Idol or America's Got Talent,* with the humor and theological depth of *Hee Haw* or *Saturday Night Live* and the excitement of a NCAA basketball championship. This church focuses primarily on entertaining us and making us feel satisfied.

In a *New Yorker* cartoon, a church is depicted with its front doors open and the congregation exiting after the worship hour. Everybody is fighting and arguing with each other. One woman is pictured hitting the minister over the head with her umbrella. A man and woman are passing by and observing this conflict. She says to him, "Goodness, I wonder what word of comfort for a troubled world the minister shared today."

Sometimes the word of God is not "Comfort ye, comfort ye my people." The word of God may need to cut into our lives with sharpness, addressing us with a "Thus saith the Lord." God's word may come to us in crass, rustic language, declaring us sinners in need of radical repentance. What entertainment do you see in the crucifixion of Jesus? And where is the warmth in Jesus' radical call to discipleship with the attendant command to go into the world and lay down your life for the cause of love?

Christ's teachings contain a sharp flint side. Christian discipleship has a sandpaper edge to it. The words of Jesus are often pointed, not always focusing on what people want but on what they need. Rather than constantly comforting his hearers, Jesus often challenged the comfortable. The prophetic words of Christ summon us to walk the more difficult way and not be content with the comforts of life.

The grace of Christ, as Bonhoeffer reminded us in word and life, is never cheap. The church of Jesus Christ aims not merely to make us feel good or tranquil or to provide us a peaceful escape from the world. The danger of a church obsessed with crowd-pleasing, entertaining, or peace-of-mind theology is that it may become a church of our own creation and not the church for which Christ died. The membership of this church is large and growing today.

The Traditional, Established, Routine, Well-Regulated, Standard, Status Quo Church of the Satisfied God

Others in America want to be members of The Traditional, Established, Routine, Well-Regulated, Standard, Status Quo Church of the Satisfied God. This church is steeped in tradition. Everything it does reaches back to ancient times. It carefully seeks to carry forward its traditions from generation to generation. There is, of course, nothing wrong with traditions, rightly used.

But in this church where change is the enemy, routine slowly becomes rut. The sameness of worship practices becomes so familiar that variety is unheard of. Set in its way, this traditional church never expects anything different to happen. God has spoken in the past, but does not continue to speak today. In this church people want nothing disturbed, nothing touched, nothing changed. They have their routine. They walk in it and do not want someone fiddling with their establishment. "Don't fix it when it ain't broke," they say. Traditions become unchangeable laws of God.

In California, there is a store called the Surprise Shop. Go into that shop, and you discover all kinds of novel items. People are happily surprised with the many and varied possibilities for purchasing. Shouldn't the church be like the Surprise Shop, open to the Holy Spirit who is breathing its new life into the church? God's church can never be totally routine, if God is constantly breaking in to surprise it with new possibilities.

Several years ago I heard Krister Stendahl, the former dean at Harvard Divinity School, speak at a church conference. He said that the contemporary church probably has all of the same problems and difficulties of the early Corinthian church except one. The church at Corinth did not suffer from the sin of dullness! Sometimes the church, regulated by its traditions, becomes deadly dull. The danger here is apathy! The danger here is a cavalier approach to eternal matters! The danger here is indifference to God's will!

A problem arose in a church in Scotland because noted poet Robert Burns lay buried in the church cemetery. Everybody in that community wanted to be buried in that cemetery with Robert Burns. Seeking to deal with the problem, the church posted a sign on the cemetery fence: "This cemetery is reserved for the dead now living in this parish."

Too often the traditional church is composed of the dead now living in it. They have no sense of aliveness to the spirit of God that is trying to break in with the freshness of God's presence and give the church new directions, new hopes, and new ways of being church. The traditional church is dead to God's spirit and very content with where it is. It is self-satisfied. It has already towed the correct line, so why disturb anything.

A wonderful story comes out of the freezing Arctic. Once the weather was so cold there that the flames on the candles froze! The explorers reached over, broke off the frozen flame of the candles, and turned them into charms. The flaming power of God, which has ignited the church in the past, has often been turned into ornaments and charms today. Many now wear a cross around their necks. The great symbols of the church have been turned into ornaments. The flaming power of Christ is not present in this kind of church. A contented church loses its power, ceases to be salt, light, and leaven in the world for Christ. The church can never be contented with where it is. God forever nudges it forward into what it can be as it is remade in God's image.

The Visionary, Pioneering Church of the Living God

Another church, thank God, exists in our land today. It is The Visionary, Pioneering Church of the Living God. This church hears an echo about its mission from the ancient psalmist (Psalm 42) who cried: "I thirst for the living God." Some scholars believe that the writer of Psalm 42 was a woman. She used the image of a female deer to begin her story. A deer is searching and groping for water. She arrives at a water hole but cannot find water. The waterhole is completely barren, so the deer leaves without satisfying her thirst. A great thirst in this woman's life had not been fulfilled. Maybe taken captive and carried into exile in Egypt, she longed to return and worship with the throngs of Israelites going up to the Jerusalem Temple to worship God. A thirst within her very being was not satisfied in that strange land, and she cried out: "I thirst for the living God."

The cry, "I thirst," is the cry of every man and woman. There is an unconscious longing within each of us. Who among us does not thirst for the presence of God? We long for the divine, knowing that the eternal alone can satisfy our real thirst. We turn to the living God, because we realize that the fountain of life is not within us. We come to the source of life. No one is totally independent and has the self-reliance to meet every situation alone. Jesus Christ is the one who said, "If any man thirst, let him come to me and drink." Jesus said to the woman at the well, "If you knew the gift of God and who it is that is saying to you, 'Give me a drink,' you would have asked him, and he would have given you living water" (John 4:10). Christ offers us the water of life that can satisfy our deepest needs. The anguished cry of every person, "I thirst for the living God," is supplied by the living God, not by material things. This longing is quenched, not by a God restricted by the past, but a God actively working in our lives.

The apostle Paul wrote that the church is a household—a family. A community of faith where brothers and sisters support and sustain one another, the church is the household of God (Ephesians 2: 19-22). The church is an assembly—*ekklesia*—the people of the living God, whether only two, three, or hundreds, gathered together to receive strength from God and one another in worship together. The Pioneering Church is a church that is the pillar and buttress of truth. It will not be frightened by truth no matter where it is encountered. It remembers that its Lord said, "You will know the truth, and the truth will make you free" (John 8:31). It is not frightened by truth from science, technology, or any other arena, because Jesus Christ has made it truly free. It will follow the path of truth wherever it leads. The church will support the truth even if every one else seeks to destroy it.

A pioneering church is always dreaming, always seeking new visions, aware that God goes before it. God constantly goes before us, leading us into deeper truths, deeper ministries, and more profound ways of being Church. John Killinger noted in his book *The Second Coming of the Church* that the church of the future may have new forms, shapes, and modes of ministry that we would not even recognize today. It may not appear to be the same institution. Killinger challenges the church to be open to God who declares that there are no limits to its possibilities. No one knows what new ideas, interpretations, or perspectives God might bring to enable the Church to follow its calling to be Christ's church in a particular community at this particular time.

At times, I have to confess, I become very discouraged as a pastor. Too many of us identify with the false churches and not the Church of the Living God. But on a depressing winter day, I used to look out my study window in Louisville, Kentucky at a large oak tree that was bare of its leaves, void of life at all. If I looked at it closely, I could see on each limb tiny, dormant buds waiting to bring life back to the tree. That tree is a living parable. God's church, filled with dormant buds, waits for the springtime of God's breath to breathe new life into it.

Don't surrender your life to The Only Understanding of Truth Church, because Jesus Christ is always breaking through our old wineskins to bring new insights and truth. It cannot contain or hold back the Living God. Don't settle for religion that is primarily entertainment, but be open to a deep, awesome worship of the Eternal God. Don't settle for the traditional, apathetic church when Christ wants to lead you into a living relationship with the God who is alive and at work in the church.

"Attend the church of your choice." Which do you choose? I hope it will be The Church of the Living God.

2

IS THE GROUND SOLID UNDER US?
THE FOUNDATION OF THE CHURCH

We all know some church buildings that are no longer used as churches. They have undergone some drastic changes. I know some church buildings that were turned into a beauty shop, a community center, a house for a family, a warehouse, and I ate in one that had been turned into a restaurant. You may know of other changes.

Steve Taylor has written a song entitled, "This Disco Used to be a Cute Cathedral." The song goes like this:

> Sell your holy habitats
> That ship's been deserted by sinking rats
> The exclusive place to go
> Is where the pious pogo
> Don't you know.
>
> This disco used to be a cute cathedral
> Where the chosen cha-cha every day of the year
> This disco used to be a cute cathedral
> Where we only play the stuff you're wanting to hear.[1]

The church has received a great deal of challenge in its history. Voices from persons like

Santayana have declared that "the shell of Christendom is broken." Swinburne, the poet, wrote that he had great admiration for Christ but despised his "leprous bride--the church." Bertrand Russell, the agnostic, once wrote: "I say quite deliberately that the Christian religion as organized in the churches has been and still is the principal enemy of moral progress in the world."

The church has indeed received a great deal of criticism from its enemies, but it has also had sharp criticism directed at it from its own friends—church leaders and theologians. I have a number of books on my shelves about the church. The titles of these books note some of the problems with today's church: *God's Frozen People, The Empty Pulpit, The Comfortable Pew, The Suburban Captivity of the Church, The Noise of Solemn Assembly, The Portrait of the Church: Warts and All, How the Church Can Minister to the World Without Losing Its Soul, The Last Days of the Church,* and *The Church of the Perfect Storm.* The church has always had to struggle to be church. In every age of the church's existence, it has struggled with the threat of the secularization of the church. The tendency is to try to mold the church into the image of society and lose sight of what Jesus intended for the church to be.

What Is the Church?

When someone asks, "What is the church?" all kinds of images come to mind. The average person might respond to the question, "What is the church?" by saying: "Well, I drive by the church on my way to work every day on Hillsborough Street or Salisbury Street or when I go downtown." Others think about the church in terms of whom the pastor is. "That is Dr. So and So's church." Some might imply that "this church is John Smith's church." They link the church with some deacon who may have been a member for years. Others say, "Let's go to church." They are talking about a building. But is the church simply a building? For two years when I was pastor of St. Matthews Baptist Church in Louisville, Kentucky, we did not have a building. Were we no longer a church when we did not have a building? That cannot be the case.

There are others who see the church as a sort of morality club. We gather occasionally, for some it is less occasionally than for others, to hear some moral talks about how we are supposed to live and what we ought to think to live correctly. From this morality club, we receive some values that we may use in our lives. Others see the church as a private club. It is for people who think alike, look alike, and act alike. These people are usually from the same socio or economic background. There are others who see the church as a social agency. They want the church to be concerned with all of the problems of society and find some remedy for them. There are others who see the church basically as a sort of theater; a place where there is music and other things that entertain. A person comes to sit and listen to a speaker, who, hopefully, will make one want to listen. They see themselves as an audience and nothing more.

The New Testament Church

Well, you think about it for a moment. Are any of these images really the church that Jesus Christ was talking about? Are they really the New Testament church? The New Testament uses numerous images for the church. Among these images are the Bride of Christ, the body of Christ, the household of faith, the family of Jehovah, the seed and shrine of the Eternal, salt, light, leaven, the vine, the temple, or the building. Paul Minear, a New Testament scholar, found more than ninety-six different images of the church in the New Testament.[2]Among this list one finds saints, disciples, believers, faithful, slaves and servant people of God, household, family, the new Exodus and the new humanity. He says that "the New Testament idea of the church is not so much a technical doctrine as a gallery of pictures." There is not just one picture, but many.

Let's stop for a moment and go back to the first mention we have of the church in the New Testament. That reference is found in the Gospel of Matthew, the sixteenth chapter. The Greek word for church, "ecclesia" (Matt. 16:18), is a word which translated means "the called out ones." The church was not so much an organization but an organism—a living group of peoples who came out from society to follow Christ. Many scholars and theologians do not believe that Jesus intended to form any kind of organization. But the other side of this question has to be raised. "Can you have any idea or ideal without some kind of organizational form of the ideal image?" The church grew out of a group of disciples who had committed themselves to Jesus Christ and, who, following Christ's resurrection, had a radical experience of faith that transformed them so fully that they began to live for him and bear witness to him.

Jesus Asked His Disciples about his Identity

Let's look for a moment at this passage from the sixteenth chapter of Matthew where Jesus paused at Caesarea Philippi and asked his disciples, "Who do men and women say that I am?" About twenty years ago I had the opportunity to stand at the place or somewhere in the region where Jesus asked his disciples this question. A deep cave is there where archaeologists have uncovered some of the images that were used in the worship of the god Pan, the god of nature. In this same area there were supposed to be fourteen temples of Baal where the Syrians worshiped their god. This area was supposed to be the source of the River Jordan which had such a significant place in the life of the nation Israel.

At this sacred place, Jesus turned to his disciples and asks, "Who are people saying I am?" Can you imagine what his disciples must have thought? "He has heard some rumors, hasn't he?" "Some are saying that he is unclean, because he has touched the blind, deaf, lame and lepers." "He has heard the rumors that some are saying that he is a sinner because he eats with sinners and has gone into their homes." "He has heard the rumors from others who questioned his right to heal, because he has no doctor's degree from Jerusalem nor does he belong to the medical society of Galilee." Others are asking,

"What are your credentials to preach? You are not in the Who's Who in Religion of Galilee. You haven't graduated from the seminary at Jerusalem. Where is your certificate of ordination? Who are you to be preaching?" "He has heard the rumors," they thought. They may have thought about all that criticism, but they say respectfully, none of those things. Instead they reply: "Some say you may be Jeremiah, Elijah, or John the Baptist returned from the dead." All of these were nice folks, prophets and forerunners of the Messiah.

Then Jesus asked the question that fell like a silver dollar dropped on a slate floor which has echoed down through the centuries and continues to echo in the lives of persons today: "Who do *You* say that I am?" That is the crucial question. "Who do YOU say that I am?" There have been all kinds of answers to that question through the years. Some of them have been almost ludicrous and others heretical. Then Simon Peter, whether responding just for himself or for the whole group of disciples, confesses, "You are the Messiah, the Christ, the Son of the living God." And what a response that was!

Christ Is the Foundation of the Church

Look at some of the key points in Matthew sixteen. We begin first with the acknowledgment that Jesus Christ is himself the foundation of the church. He is the foundation. As Paul says in 1 Corinthians 3:11: "For no one can lay any foundation other than the one that has been laid; that foundation is Jesus Christ." Jesus says: "I will build my church." "*I* will build." Jesus Christ is the foundation stone. In Ephesians, Paul writes about Jesus as "the chief cornerstone" of the church (Eph.3:20). When asked for a sign of his authority, Jesus used an interesting image. "Destroy this temple,"—and he wasn't talking about the physical Jewish temple but he was speaking about himself—"and in three days I will raise it up" (John 2:19). The Jews misunderstood Jesus and thought he was speaking about the temple in Jerusalem. But John declares that Jesus was speaking not about a building made of stone but his own body which his enemies would destroy but would be raised on the third day (John 2:21C22). John had said earlier, "The Word became flesh and 'tabernacled' among us" (John 1:14). His body was the new temple. He was to incorporate the new Israel, the new humanity. He is the foundation of the church.

In Corinthians 15:20:27 Paul underscores that the risen Lord is the foundation of the church. "If Christ be not raised, then our faith is in vain," Paul said. But Christ is risen (1 Cor.15:15-17). Jesus Christ is himself the foundation of the church. All else is sinking sand.

The Church Is Christ's Possession

Secondly, the church is Christ's possession. The Church belongs to its Lord. Jesus said, "I will build *my* church." The church is never yours or mine. The church is always under the Lordship of Jesus Christ. Christ is Lord or it is not church. Wherever Jesus Christ is, there is the church. If Jesus Christ is not present, it doesn't make any difference what kind of building, programs, preachers, choirs or anything else we may have, it is not the church.

I heard about a business meeting in another church where I was not pastor, thank goodness! The church was likely engaged in an argument about what color the carpet was going to be, what section of the church would be covered or on which side of the church the piano went. Finally one deacon rose up in anger and exclaimed; "I don't care what the Christian thing is. This is what I want!" Do you hear that? We get so much of that in church. "I don't care what the Christian thing is to do or what Christ wants. I want my way." Instead of searching the Scriptures to know the mind of Christ, we want our way.

The Importance of Faith Commitment

Thirdly, the church is built on the confession of believers. In this story in Matthew's Gospel, we read about Peter's confession of faith. Peter made a confession of faith in his recognition that Jesus was the Christ. Peter's confession has been a storm-center of the Church down through the ages. Catholics and Protestants have usually been on opposite sides. Some have tried to solve the problem by referring to the Greek language and noting a play on words in the Greek name for Peter and the Greek word for rock which are very similar. This view attempts to place the emphasis on Peter's faith and not on Peter. But Jesus didn't speak Greek, he spoke Aramaic. In Aramaic the word for Peter and rock are the same word.

What was Jesus saying when he stated: "You are Peter and upon you I will build by Church?" The

Church is built on the confession of Peter. He was the first stone which was built on the foundation stone—Jesus Christ. He was the first to recognize that Jesus Christ was Lord. He became the first stone in the Church. The apostles became the other stones in the foundation of the Church by their confession of faith. All other Christians, through their confessions down through the years have become a part of the foundation of the Church. The Church was built on Peter's confession, the disciples' confession and your confession and on mine. The Church was built on each of them and each of us. It is your confession and the confession of other disciples that are a part of the "body" of Christ's church. It is the confession of every Christian down through the ages that makes up the church. All of us are a part of this body.

Jesus was not just the founder of a religion. He is its foundation. He is its source. "I, if I be lifted up," Jesus declared. "I will draw all men (and women) unto me." "I am the way, the truth, and the life. No one comes to the Father but by me." Jesus did not ask his followers, "Do you believe in God?" or "Do you think the Beatitudes are correct?" No! He put himself at the center of his message. "Come unto me." "Follow me." "Believe me." "Learn of me." "Preach in my name."

"Who do you say that I am?" The New Testament rings with the words that men said about him and claims Jesus made for himself. He is the Son of David, Son of God, Son of man, Messiah, the Servant of God, the Good Shepherd, the Divine Physician, the Savior, the Prophet, King, the Stone,

Bridegroom, the Bread of Life, the Light of the World, the Door, the Vine, the Way, the Truth, the Life, the Resurrection and the Life, the Judge, the Lamb, the Scapegoat, the High Priest, the Just One, the Amen, the Alpha and Omega, the Beginning and End, the Head, the Image, the Christ of Creation, the Firstborn of Creation, the Bright and Morning Star, and others.

You can't be Christian and not be related to Jesus Christ. There has to be the confession that Jesus is Lord. This is the central foundation stone in the church for the believer. Oh, I know that we are sometimes criticized in the church because we refer so often to Jesus. This reminds me about the small boy whose Sunday School teacher asked her class one Sunday: "What is it that climbs a tree, is furry, and has a bushy tail?" The little boy looked up and said, "Because I am in Sunday School I know I should say Jesus. But it really sounds like a squirrel to me." I know we struggle with that concern sometimes in church. But, dear friends, Jesus Christ is our basic confession of faith. Confession in Christ is the foundation for bringing believers together, or we are not church.

The Church's Foundation Is Secure

Fourthly, we find that the foundation of the church is secure, because it is on solid ground. Jesus said, "The gates of hell shall not prevail against it" (Matt. 16:18). The gates of Hades were a very familiar metaphor to the Jewish people. They were symbolic of the forces of evil and the powers of death. Jesus knew that his disciples would go through misunderstanding, rejection, and persecution. The followers of Jesus Christ have always had to withstand persecutions and rejections. Many have thought they could stamp out the Church. Others have seen the Church as so inept that they thought it could not survive. The Church was seen by many as being so corrupt in the fifteenth century that there seemed to be no possibility for survival. But then, Martin Luther came on the scene, and the Church was reformed. There were many who thought that the Church in England in the nineteenth century was dead, and Wesley began to preach and the Church was transformed. Many Christians thought that the Church would never be missionary minded again, but then along came William Carey, and there was a rebirth in the Church. The scandals of Pedophilia in the Roman Catholic Church and the sex scandals in many Protestant churches have many wondering about the church today. Who will come along and give guidance through this wilderness?

God is constantly coming into the life of his people and breathing new life into the Church. There are those in our own day who are frightened that the church is going to be swallowed up in secularism or caught up in a mentality that will totally distort it. But thank goodness there are voices who are willing to stand up and challenge these modern corruptions and say, "This is not the authentic church." Let's hear again what Jesus said his Church would be and not buy any distortion of it.

A Commission to Serve

Then we receive, in the fifth place, a commission from Jesus. Jesus said to Peter, "I will give to you the keys of the kingdom of heaven" (Matt. 16:19). That phrase has caused a lot of misunderstanding in the Church. What is Jesus telling him? He is saying: "You are to be a steward in my kingdom." A steward is someone who manages and administers the affairs of someone else, "The keys to the success of my kingdom's work are in your hands. I will be leaving soon, Peter, you are responsible for sharing my love and grace with others. Whether or not it is successful is in your hands. You are my steward. Carry on my gospel and pass the good news onto others. It is up to you." This seems to be the basic emphasis here. The keys were passed to Peter, the other disciples and to every believer through the centuries.

The Church today is at a crossroads. We can be grateful for our past and build on it and move forward or we can look back and say, "The good old days are gone forever." We can be nostalgic and wish we were like we were in the 50's or 60's, the 80's 90's or the first part of the 2000's or we can dream about our possibilities for the future, new shapes and ministries for service, new goals to share Christ with a new age, and not try to confine our message to the image of what some call the good old days.

Instead we can help construct the church toward the good new days. Let us not be frightened by the future, but be aware that Christ always goes before us. Let the church affirm its many strengths, its rich history and heritage, many attractive places of worship with various styles and kinds of worship services from high church, traditional to commentary, many good, functional buildings, strong, dedicated ministerial staffs in many churches, a variety of gifts in our laypersons, many with a strong sense of mission and a desire to serve, with wonderful ministries and programs in most of our churches, good financial resources in many congregations, many churches with thinking congregation with an openness to new insights, and many churches committed to women/men in ministry, and many more. Let's build on our strengths. Let's light torches for the future and walk in their light.

Now it is up to you and to me to carry the message to others. The "keys to the kingdom" have been passed down through the centuries by others until they have reached you, and now they are in your hands. Have you ever been house hunting and finally came upon a house that you wanted to see? You may have walked up the steps and discovered a sign in the window: "Key next door." You, then, had to go next door to get the key to get in. There are a lot of Christians who want to pass the key next door. But the key is in your hands and in my hands. We are stewards of the Gospel of Christ. We who have received so much are now challenged and commissioned to share this love with other people. Friends, if you and I have been called to be a part of the Church of Christ, he has placed a key in the hand of every single one of us to share the good news of Christ with others. That is our commission.

A Brief Summary

If I could summarize what I think are the biblical concepts of church, I would list these characteristics in six summary statements. First, the church came into existence as God's gift and not by human achievement. Second, the church is not a physical institution but a fellowship of believers. Third, the church by its nature as body is not individual but corporate. When we are only concerned about our own individual wants in church, we miss the point. The church is the body-- corporate. We have to be concerned about the whole church. Faith is never private. It is personal, but not private. Fourth, the church is not limited to a local congregation but is universal. Fifth, the church is not the depository of some wonderful memory about Christ but is the place where the living Lord dwells. Sixth, the church does not exist for its own sake but for the glory of God. Whenever the church becomes so concerned about its own perpetuation, it loses sight of what it was created to be as church.

Several years ago at Actor's Theater in Louisville, Kentucky, I saw a play entitled *To Culebra*, about Ferdinand Delesseps, who directed the construction of the Suez Canal and, in his later years planned the construction of the Panama Canal. His company went bankrupt trying to dig the canal. One day he was talking to his son about his work, "You must always remember," he said, "that the pessimists are the spectators of life."

Many people become discouraged easily and turn away from their goals. Negative and critical attitudes cast discouragement in the paths of others. Anybody can throw stumbling blocks in another's path. What stepping stones do you provide? Anybody can throw obstacles in the way. What helping hands do you extend? When we make the faith attractive, we draw men and women to Christ.

A man, who recently joined a church, said: "I haven't been this excited about a church for years." When we are excited about the faith and our church's ministry in spreading the gospel, we will share this experience with others.

If we do not make the faith attractive to others, especially in church, who will be drawn to the church? Then we are so content individualistically on having "my" way and not on what is best for the Church, how sad is our understanding of church. My prayer is that whoever joins a particular church's fellowship will grow in the faith and not be hindered by that fellowship but strengthened and encouraged by it. We should strive to make every local church Christ's Church. Remember that the Church is never the pastor's church, a deacon's church, some lay person's church nor your church or mine. It is Christ's church! Let us affirm that as we follow the Lord of the Church.

[1] http://www.lyricsmania.com

[2] Paul Minear, *Images of the Church in The New Testament* (Philadelphia: Westminster Press, 1960).

3.

WHAT DO WE DO UNDER THAT BIG ROOF?

The Church at Worship

Several years ago I had the opportunity to talk with a group of boys and girls in one of my former churches who came in to look at our church sanctuary. One of the youngsters in the group looked up and asked; "Hey, Mr. Pastor, what goes on under this big roof?"

Well, what does go on under this big roof? This big roof was designed as a place where we could worship God. Archaeologists who have examined the ruins of various civilizations state that they have discovered three basic things: an altar, a prison, and a cemetery. The altar indicates that men and women worshiped. A prison indicates that people have sinned. A cemetery denotes that men and women die. In the ruins of every civilization, worship has been a key factor.

You may have heard about the young girl who came to her mother and asked: "Mother, you know the vase that you told us had been passed on down through the generations in the family?" "Yes," the mother said, "I know about that, daughter. That is one of my most prized possessions." "Well, I hate to tell you," the daughter continues, "but this generation has dropped it." There are a lot of people in this generation who have dropped worship. They have not made it a vital part of their lives and that is a tragedy.

Isaiah's Vision of Worship

For guidance in our worship, let us turn to the sixth chapter of the Book of Isaiah. Here are some significant characteristics of worship. In the year that King Uzziah died, which was approximately 736 B.C., Isaiah went to the temple to worship. This was a time of great sorrow for Isaiah, because Uzziah had been a very beloved king. Uzziah was only sixteen years old when he began his reign and was on the throne for about fifty years. He had been a good king and it was a prosperous time for Israel. His death ushered in a crisis for the nation. Isaiah's reaction to Uzziah's death may have been similar to the feelings many persons experienced when president Franklin Delano Roosevelt died in 1945. He had served as president from 1933 until his death in 1945. He was the only president many had ever known and was greatly beloved by many. For another generation, the death of President John F. Kennedy produced great trauma, as they wondered how fragile our government might be.

The Call to Adoration

In his time of sorrow Isaiah went to the temple to worship. In that worship experience Isaiah had a vision which changed his life. His vision of God contained three basic elements. The first was a vision of God and the call to adoration. "I saw the Lord high and lifted up." The whole foundation of the temple began to shake. Although the king was dead, Isaiah was assured that the eternal God was not dead. We need that same assurance.

Isaiah experienced the majesty of God which was so overwhelming to him that the train of God's robe, his presence, filled the whole temple. The folds of God's royal robe filled the whole temple and six seraphim, "the burning ones," in Hebrew, surrounded God whose majesty was indescribable and whose being was clothed in unapproachable mystery and wonder. These seraphim, creatures of "flame and light," stood over or above the Lord, who was seated on his throne, to render continuous worship and service.

The Holiness of God

Isaiah experienced the holiness of God. In his vision, Isaiah heard the seraphim as they sang to God: "Holy, Holy, Holy." The seraphim had six wings. With two of the wings, they covered their eyes; with two, they covered their feet, and with two, they flew. They covered their eyes and face out of their sense of reverence for God. They covered their feet, or really better translated their genital organs, to hide their nakedness before God because of their humility. With the other two wings they flew, which indicated their way of serving God. Through his vision of the angels of God, Isaiah depicted concepts of reverence, humility, and service.

As he saw God high and lifted up, Isaiah heard the angel sing: "Holy, Holy, Holy." The word holy means that God is separate. God is the one above us. Our sins separate us from him. We are the ones who have come to worship him. We seek to restore our broken relationship. The effect of the presence of God in the temple caused the threshold or foundation of the whole building to shake. When God's spirit permeates our being, our whole life should feel the shaking effect of his presence. A vision of God does not leave our life the same again.

For Isaiah this experience of the holiness of God was so intense that it forever shaped his ministry. God was to him forever grand and wondrous beyond compare. He constantly denounced the pride of the people. He called them to fall down before the holiness of God and not cling to their sinful pride (Is. 2:12-22 for example).

When Moses stood before the burning bush, God said to him, "Take off your shoes, because the ground on which you stand is holy ground." I wonder what we would do today if we had such an experience. Well, we would probably want a camera or a video camera to take a picture of the burning bush. Rather than taking off our shoes in worship, we might want to sell popcorn or candy to entertain people. Rather than taking off our shoes, we would probably want to prop our feet up someplace and discuss why we think the burning bush is not consumed. What am I saying? Many today have lost the sense of the holiness of God. I know in my own experience that my awareness of the holiness of God permeates my whole concept of what worship is. We bow before God, who is wholly and holy other than we. We always seek to bring God our very best in worship and bow in humility before God.

A Lack of Preparation

Sometimes we have difficulty in worshiping God because we make no preparation for our worship. We come in the church door, sit in our pew and continue chatting even after the organist begins to play. We talk about all sorts of things in the world without directing our thoughts toward God at all. The Jewish people began their worship on the night before the Sabbath. They paused to get ready for worship. Maybe we, too, need to learn better how to make preparation for it. I have a friend who said that the moment he put his hand on the door at church, he began to focus his mind in a deliberate way on how he might worship God.

Spectators in Worship

One of our biggest problems with worship today, however, is that many want only to be spectators in their worship. People are content to be an audience instead of worshipers. It is very difficult really to worship when we are merely an audience. Religious television has really hurt us here. They have made us into onlookers and spectators in religion. There is an interesting book; written by Quinton Schultze entitled *Televangelism and American Culture: The Business of Popular Religion*. He underscores the damage of televangelism in these words:

> *The result of televangelists' capitulation to the popular culture and to the intrinsic demands of the medium is the substitution of the new message for the old evangel. This message focuses primarily on the personality and authority of the evangelist; substitutes entertainment for nurture and sorcery for evangelism; transforms believers into an audience; tells viewers what they want to hear rather than what they need to hear; turns the gospel into a product and evangelism into marketing; equates spiritual faithfulness with financial support; and sets ministry against ministry in competition for audience share.[1]*

The religious shows of televangelists are one of the heresies of our age, and we need to fight this heresy with every ounce of our strength. They have made worship personality centered—and by that I mean the personality of the preacher instead of God-centered. Whenever the attention of worship focuses on the preacher, the musicians, organists or some other person instead of God, the direction is all wrong. All the persons in the service should point clearly to God and not seek to draw attention to themselves. We need to remember that worship is not primarily what you and I get out of it. But it is what we bring to God. God is not so much seeking to satisfy your need or my need, as we are seeking to satisfy God. Worship is not something that God does for us. Worship is what we do for God. That is a key which many of us have lost. Isaiah saw God high and lifted up. He experienced the sovereignty of God. God's throne was above all else. The sovereign Ruler of the world was still reigning.

Worship Challenges Us to Look at Ourselves

Secondly, Isaiah had a vision about himself. He came to worship in a time of great national sorrow. He may have had doubts and suffered from depression. We don't know. How many times do we say, "I can't worship if I am not in the mood for it." We may be depressed, lonely, sad, be low or be affected by our moods, but remember worship is not controlled by our mood. God broke through Isaiah's grieving mood and gave him a vision of his presence. In his experience of worship, Isaiah discovered his own sinfulness. "Woe is me. I am unclean," he cried. The holiness of God helped him see that he was sinful.

Awareness of Our Sins

Today many people do not want to hear about their sins. They want to come to church and be happy and feel good. They do not want somebody to make them aware that they are sinners. The positive thinking and possibility thinking philosophy of some television evangelists make us think we are OK. These television preachers seldom speak about sin or the cross. But this passage reminds us that when we meet the Holy God, we are confronted as sinners and in need of redemption.

In one of Charles Schultz's cartoons, Lucy walks over to Snoopy and places a balloon in his mouth and says: "I am going in for lunch, Snoopy...Hold this for me..." "Whatever you do," she says, "Don't let go of it." In a few moments, he falls asleep. Several frames show Snoopy sleeping and, then, all of a sudden he gives a big yawn. As he opens his mouth and yawns, the balloon floats off into the air. In the last caption you see him with a little sack on a stick, looking like a hobo, and walking down the railroad track saying: "Make one mistake and you pay for it the rest of your life." But the Christian gospel does not leave us trapped in our past mistakes. God offers us forgiveness and opportunity to begin anew.

The Power of Forgiveness

One of the beautiful symbols in this passage is the purging of Isaiah's sinfulness with a coal taken from the altar of God. His lips are purged by the touch of that coal upon them. This symbol reminds us that forgiveness is not easy or painless. The forgiveness of sins is not without pain. To confess to someone that you have hurt them, wronged them, betrayed them, or let them down is painful. The forgiveness of God sometimes brings us suffering and hurt. God's spirit will bring us forgiveness and purges us from our sins and makes us whole but this experience may be painful.

It is also interesting to me that Isaiah cried out "I have unclean lips" rather than an unclean heart. But isn't it often true that our lips reveal what is in our heart? And since Isaiah was to be a spokesman for God he had to have his lips purged so that he could declare the authentic truth of God. When our lips are purged, it symbolizes that our inner life has also been purged and changed.

Some people try to focus on a tangent of worship instead of its central thrust. This kind of selective focus is seen in the conversation which Jesus had with the Samaritan woman by the city's well. She began by trying to go off on a tangent. She noted that the Samaritans worshiped God over on one mountaintop and the Jews worshiped on another mountain. "Where are we really supposed to worship anyway?" she asked. The Samaritans had been very selective in their view of the Scriptures. They believed that the only part of the Scripture which was authentic was the Pentateuch, the first five books in the Old Testament. They rejected the Prophets, and the wisdom literature. They were very selective in what they believed was the word of God. This, of course, led to a very selective approach to worship as well.

We Can Encounter God Anywhere

Notice what Jesus told the Samaritan woman about worship. "You shall worship God in spirit and truth." Place is not an end in itself. Hopefully, we shall not permit the beautiful symbols in this place, or any place of worship, to become an end in themselves. All of our worship symbols point us to God. They should never get in the way of our communing with God. Architecturally and symbolically our sanctuary seeks to point us to sense God, who is high and lifted up and to worship him within the very depths of our being. We gather that we might have a vision of God. We come with our mind, our heart, and our spirit open to the power of his presence.

There are many people today who want to pick and choose how God addresses them. Some believe that unless God comes down a particular mental street, one cannot encounter God. They will not be open to God except in a certain place. There are some who have so preprescribed God's domain of worship that unless God walks back down the aisle of their little country church, they cannot worship. Unless God communicates to them through a Fifth Avenue Sanctuary, they cannot hear God's voice. Unless they have a certain choir, or a particular kind of music, or a particular form of worship, or a particular preaching style, God can't communicate with them. This attitude tries to limit God's presence to the known and familiar. That is unfortunate because God's spirit, like the wind, blows where it will. I confess that I understand this attitude. I often face that same kind of struggle and I am very uncomfortable in some kind of worship settings.

Jesus reminded the woman at the well that God is spirit, and he can communicate with us in many places, means and ways. As we gather to worship, God may come to meet us in familiar places or in new "wineskins" that we cannot anticipate or might expect. We must open our lives to encounter God in spirit and truth and acknowledge that we cannot pigeonhole God in any of our narrow places, creeds, dogma or traditions. God often breathes through these old forms, but the breath of God's presence may open new doors and windows in our perception of God's presence.

A Call to Service

Finally, worship gives us, as it did Isaiah, a vision of responsibility and service. After Isaiah had experienced the holiness of God, where he had seen God high and lifted up, and then experienced the forgiveness of God's grace when he realized his own sense of inadequacy, then he heard God ask, "Whom shall I send? Who will go for me?" Isaiah responded; "Here am I. Send me."

When we gather to worship, our central affirmation is that it is not so much we who are seeking God as God is always seeking us. God is the eternal pursuer who continues to trail us down through the ages of time to come into your life and my life and bring us his love and grace. God pursues us. He comes to us and draws us to himself. Having experienced God in our lives, we then should be different because of that encounter. Worship should make a difference in our lives. If we leave church Sunday after Sunday and there is no real difference in our lives, have we really worshiped God? When we meet the living God of the universe in worship, we should go out and live, think, and act differently because of that meeting.

Remain Open to God

When the God of the universe came into Isaiah's life, he heard God's voice: "Who will go?" And he responded: "Here am I, send me," Out of our meeting with God in worship, we exclaim: "I will go, Lord, and I will live for you in all of my life." We should not be the same. When God has come into our life, we should be radically different. Worship calls us to a high hill, a holy place, in which we sense God high and lifted up. The vision from that elevation enables us to see life in a new perspective. From the hilltop with God, we should go back down into the valleys of life and be strengthened to face the problems and difficulties more effectively. Our relationship with the eternal God of the universe fortifies us to refocus our whole purpose about living. Our perspective changes from getting to giving, serving instead of getting.

If you and I have a real genuine experience with God, we cannot be spectators. We cannot be content with being an audience. God demands participation. When we participate in worship, we are drawn into a relationship where we sense our own sins; we experience forgiveness, and having experienced forgiveness, then God challenges us to rise up to serve him. We can't be spectators. We are called to ministry.

There is a Methodist church in Chicago which claims to be the tallest Methodist church in the world. Above the church building is a tall skyscraper office building and above the office building is a tall slender steeple. The church decided that they ought to do something a bit more religious to bear witness to their community, so they decided to install some bells in their steeple. Then around the clock and on the hour, the crowds on the streets below might hear them and want to come to worship. The bells were installed. But then when they rang the bells in the high steeple, noise of the traffic, the busy, rushing people and the far distance of the bells above the people made them inaudible. They rang the bells, but nobody could hear them. The distance was too great and the people were too busy.

Sometimes our busyness, anxiety, involvement in everything else—our distance from God—keeps us from hearing God's voice calling to us. The most important thing we do as church is worship. Everything else we do stems from that experience. If we really do not worship God, then we will not serve God.

Worship Is Essential

If we have really met God in worship—had a "vision" of God—then we will want to come again and again to this place of worship. We cannot do without worship. This is the place we experience God's forgiveness, love, grace, peace and guidance. When we allow everything else to push worship aside, then we are acknowledging that to us it is not essential.

Yet, worship is as essential to real living as food to survival, water to quench our thirst, air for breathing, light for seeing and sound for hearing. Worship is the most important act we do to nourish our spiritual life. To fail in worship is to cut one's self off from God.

Isaiah encountered God in a special way that forever changed his life. I pray that each of us will have a similar experience. Our faithfulness in worship will reflect our commitment. Let us gather to reverence and adore God, make our confession of sin, experience God's forgiving grace, and accept our commission to serve God in our daily lives.

[1]Quentin J. Schultze, *Televangelism and American Culture: The Business of Popular Religion*, (Grand Rapids: Baker, 1991)

4.

How Are We Going to Run This Thing?

The Gifts of Ministry Within the Church

Some years ago I read a story about Michelangelo. He was seen transporting a large piece of marble on a wagon down a road. A curious peasant nearby looked up and in a lazy way asked him, "Why are you struggling so hard with that big old piece of rock?" "There is an angel inside that rock," Michelangelo responded, "who wants to get free."

One of the essential ministries of the church is to help its members set their spiritual gifts free. There is a wide variety of gifts within the church, and a part of the charge which the church has is to help set these gifts free in people. How are we going to run the church? The church should function today the same way that our Lord intended it to be run when he founded it--by the gifts of those who are his disciples. As each Christian contributes his or her gifts in ministry to our Lord, the work of the church will be accomplished.

A Variety of Spiritual Gifts

Paul stresses in Ephesians 4:7, 11-12 and 1 Corinthians 12: 1-13 that there are a variety of spiritual gifts. This has been true from the very beginning of the church. Look at the first disciples. Simon Peter was radically different from John. Peter had great gifts of leadership but at times he displayed an impulsive spirit, a fiery temper and sometimes he was courageous. On other occasions he was cowardly and indecisive. Thomas was the disciple who came to a deep faith only through his questions, doubts and fears. John, the beloved disciple, was loving, gentle and quiet. Andrew was the disciple who served behind the scenes. He was always friendly, not seeking recognition, and was always introducing others to Jesus. Mary and Martha were so different in their personalities. One was concerned about the preparation of food; the other with learning at her Master's feet. Paul arose on the scene, nurtured with his rabbinic scholarship. Without question, he was a leader and organizer but at times he was arrogant and uncompromising, at other times gentle and loving, courageous and bold. Mary Magdalene celebrated her gift of service even to the point of public embarrassment that she might wash the feet of Jesus. The early church began by drawing on the diverse gifts of those first believers.

In Ephesians and 1 Corinthians and in several other passages of Scripture, the variety of spiritual gifts is clearly noted. In Romans 12:6-8, Paul mentions seven different gifts. The gifts he lists here are prophecies, service, teaching, exhortation, giving or contributing, leadership and mercy. In 1Corinthians 12:8-10 there is an additional listing of wisdom, knowledge, faith, healing, miracles, discerning of spirits, tongues, interpretation, apostle, helps, and administration. In the fourth chapter of Ephesians there are two other gifts which are added—evangelist and pastor. Prophecy is mentioned in all three references. Prophecy is not so much telling what will happen in the future as "forth telling" today what the word of God is in judgment upon us. Teacher is mentioned in Romans and again in Ephesians. Most of the twenty are only mentioned one time. In I Peter 4:10-11 there are some additional words about gifts.

Are these all of the spiritual gifts? I do not think so. This list is not an exhaustive list of all possible spiritual gifts. This list notes the particular gifts which were necessary to meet the needs in the life of the young church at that time. Special gifts should not be narrowly confined to these items. Paul often gave a different listing himself. The situation in Rome, Corinth, and Ephesus would be different and demanded different gifts. Even from the beginning, the church had a variety of gifts.

Diversity of Gifts

Rather than these gifts being merely incidental, it is likely that our Lord intended that diversity be a part of the nature of the church. All Christians were not supposed to be alike. We all bring differing gifts to God to perform different functions. As someone once observed, "There is no one best way to do everything." Throughout the twelfth chapter of Corinthians, Paul stresses the diversity and inter-dependence of these gifts. All gifts are important in God's sight and God seeks to draw out the gifts within the believers.

The church recognizes that all Christians have gifts. Some may be more gifted than others, but every single Christian has some gift that he or she can utilize in ministry for Christ. Several years ago Emily, my wife, and I were in a circle along with others at a church function. The leader said to me: "Bill, would you take Emily's place?" "No," I responded, "I can't do that. I will change seats with her, but I can't take her place." I can't take her place. She has her gifts and I have mine. The church must acknowledge the gifts which others have. As Romans 12:6 states, "Having gifts that differ accordingly to the grace given us, let us use them."

Provoking Gifts

One of the ministries of the church is to help provoke the gifts within us so they can be used in service for Christ. How do we discover these gifts? The Church of the Savior, in Washington, D.C., has in the membership statement of their church that the church is a ship on which "there are no passengers--all are crew members." One of the basic purposes of the church, as they understand it, is to evoke the gifts which people have so they will be used in service for Christ. No one can be a member of that church and not use his or her gift in some ministry. Each person must discover what his or her gift is and use it. Sadly, in too many of our churches, people do not even know what their gifts are, and if they do know what they are, many of them are unwilling to use them. In a true church, there can be no spectators—all are participants in ministry.

Gordon Cosby, pastor of the Church of the Savior, observes three ways people can learn to discover their spiritual gifts. The *first* way you discover your gifts is with a sense of *eureka*. Ah! A light goes on within, and you feel a strong sense of excitement and satisfaction about this discovery. *Secondly*, you begin to dream about what you can do with that gift in ministry. Then *thirdly*, you realize that you have got to talk about it because it is so important to you. Sometimes there are responsibilities we all do in church that we don't have a sense of *eureka* about. Every time we do something in church does not mean that we will always find it exciting. We may at first have to discover what our gifts are by trying various tasks so our gifts can be developed. We can be taught to grow in an area so our gifts can be nurtured and improved. Sometimes our work may be a burden, feel like an obligation, or be difficult, or at times even painful. But God has not promised us that our service would always be easy. We might even fail at some of our tasks. But we may need to explore a number of possibilities before we discover what our gifts are and how we can use them in ministry for Christ. In a Gallup poll it was determined that "too many individuals talents and strengths were underutilized."[1] The church needs to make a concerted effort to draw upon the wealth of its personal resources.

Discovering Gifts

One of the church's tasks is to help you discover your gift and then try to help you find how you might use that gift in service for Christ. Yes, there are a variety of gifts. There is not only one way of serving Christ. What are some of the spiritual gifts that we might see today in the church? Among these gifts might be biblical scholars, theologians, church musicians, administrators, missionaries, dramatists, artists, writers, journalist, counselors, social workers or preachers. The list is endless. There is no end to the variety of gifts that can be used as they are called forth in service for Christ.

All spiritual gifts do not have to be used within a church building. We need many gifts to carry on the functions within a church building. Over five hundred persons served in many different ways in St. Matthews Baptist Church when I served as its pastor. And I know that it takes hundreds to do the ministries of this church. However, many people will use their spiritual gifts in the world for God. If our gifts are not used in the world, then we may be failing more there than any place else. For example, the gift of evangelism ought to be used in the world to bear witness to God's saving grace. This gift is best used not in the church, but in the world, outside the doors of the church building. We are also challenged to minister in the world to the poor, hungry, sick, the homeless and help overcome racism, injustice, crime, disease and other problems. First of all our texts tell us that there are a variety of spiritual gifts. We are not all alike, nor gifted alike. Let's recognize that fact and be grateful.

All Gifts Come From God

Paul goes further and reminds us that all gifts come from God. We receive these gifts by the grace of God. Much of what we have has come as a gift from God. God created the world and we receive this gift of creation. Salvation is God's gift. "For God so loved the world that he gave...." (John 3:16). Handel wrote about that this way, "Unto us a Son is given." God's gift of his Son is a wonderful gift that we have to receive. Much of life comes to us as a gift from God. The sunshine, rain, air we breathe, our own lives are all gifts from God. We have to assimilate, discover, motivate, train and guide ourselves in the use of these gifts. First, however, we must acknowledge that they are indeed gifts.

Not a Call for Pride

As we affirm our gifts from God, this should not issue in a sense of pride. We should have a feeling of joy that we can use what gifts we have in ministry for God. Some people say they do not want to discover their gift, because it might be an expression of pride. Well, there is no question that there is a real difference between spiritual gifts and human talents. Flaunting one's talent for personal reasons can be an expression of pride. To utilize your spiritual gift for God is to recognize that your gift is to be used not for self glory but to glorify God. I seek not to call attention to myself with my gift but recognize that I have been converted by God, therefore, I am directing my gift to use in ministry for God. This is a real difference. I have discovered my spiritual gift after I have been converted, and I dedicate that gift to God. If my desire is to use my gift for my own selfish goal or that I might receive gratification and praise from persons, then I have missed the point. My gift is not for self glory but was given to me so I might glorify and praise God. Spiritual gifts are misused if they are focused on one's own person. We are to point others to God, not to seek more recognition for ourselves.

The church seeks to affirm the spiritual gifts in its members. What are the gifts that have been affirmed in your life by others? Let me pick out one individual for an example. I might note some of the gifts the church has affirmed in the Minister of Music in the church where I am pastor. Clearly the church has acknowledged her musical gifts, administration, teaching, writing, the warmth of her personality, and others. From time to time our church has recognized the spiritual gifts of many other members and affirmed them. We all could make a long list of gifts we have seen in various individuals in our particular congregations. I have felt the affirmation within my own life of certain gifts which various churches and other congregations have affirmed in my life. Each of us seeks to dedicate his or her gifts to God, because we realize that all gifts come from God.

One year when I was pastor at St. Matthews Baptist Church in Louisville, Kentucky, we had a deacons' retreat at the Sisters of Charity Center at Nazareth, Kentucky. In a small chapel there are some beautiful stained glass windows. On one side of the chapel, the windows represent God's gifts to humanity. These gifts are depicted as creation, nativity, crucifixion, resurrection and Pentecost. On the other side of the chapel are some windows which depict what the nuns say are their gifts to God. These gifts are teaching, nursing, obedience, chastity, and poverty. In Nazareth, Kentucky, a small group of women have served God since about 1850 as nurses, teachers, and spiritual guides. They have offered their gifts in service for God in that part of Kentucky. Like these dedicated women, each of us needs to acknowledge that his or her gifts come from God and are to be used for God's glory.

Gifted for the Unity of the Church

Paul was also bold to affirm that these gifts are to be used for the unity of the church. One of the saddest things about the church today is that persons often use their gifts to fragment the church instead of unifying it. Can you imagine accepting the call to a church where there was a four-way faction in the church? Yet Paul went to the Corinthian church to try to heal such a division. Within that church, there were those who wanted to follow the leadership of Apollos, others rallied around Simon Peter, others Paul and others said they just wanted to follow Christ. In writing to the Corinthian Church, Paul was striving for the unity of the church. He wanted to end a four-way split and get the people together. Paul saw disunity as one of the worst things that could happen in a church. Paul felt that anyone who tried to use their gifts to divide the fellowship and bring about fragmentation or cause problems were working against Christ whose body they were supposed to be.

One in Service

The Church is Christ's body. Just as the human body is diverse and inter-related, so is the church. The human body cannot say, "Well, I am the hand, so I am more important than the foot." Or, "I am the ear and I am more important than the eye." All parts are important to the work of the whole. The human body has many different parts: eyes, ears, feet, hands, etc., and all are important to the functioning of the body. If the body parts were at war with one another, we would destroy our body. We need to be unified. The Church is supposed to be one in serving Christ. Every Christian is to work for the unity of the body. If we are working against the unity of the body, we are not seeking to do the will of Christ. We are working against him. Jesus laid down his life for the church, and as the church represents the body of Christ, who was the Incarnation of God, so we seek to carry on his ministry through his body, the church today.

Bill Staines has written a folk song entitled, "A Place in the Choir." "All God's critters get a place in the choir, some sing low, some sing higher, some sing out loud on the telephone wire and some just clap their hands or paws." All have a place in the choir. Staines is stressing the place everyone has in God's creation. We all have a place in God's grand design. All of us have a part in God's great orchestra—the church. We need to let our gift be used in building up the unity of the church.

All Gifts Are Important

In working for the unity of the church, we recognize that no ministry in God's sight is higher or lower than another. A part of the struggle which Paul saw in the Corinthian church was with those who thought their gifts were better than others. Some thought because they could speak in tongues, they were superior to others in their gifts. Some may have thought that a pastor, an apostle, or some other gift was superior. Paul's analogy of the variety of the parts of the human body was to affirm the diversity and importance of every part. All spiritual gifts are important to God. None ranks higher than another. All are important.

Karl Barth, the noted theologian, brought this into clear focus when he observed:

> *There can be no talk of higher and lower orders of specific services. There is differentiation of functions, but the preacher cannot really stand any higher than the other elders, nor the bell-ringer any lower than the professor of theology. There can be no "clergy" and no "laity," no merely "teaching" and no merely "listening" Church, because there is no member of the Church who is not the whole thing in his (or her) place.*[2]

Every single one of us is an important part of the body of Christ. Our goal is to work for unity. If we are doing anything to work against the unity, then we don't understand what the church is. We are seeking to unify the body as we use our gift as a part of the whole. Our goal is never to be divisive, but to be part of the unity— the whole.

Our Gifts Are for Service

Paul reminds the Corinthians that our gifts are to be used (Rom. 12:6; Eph. 4:12). We are not to bury our gift in the ground like the man who had only one talent. We are not to bury our gift within ourself. We are to use our gift for "the building up of the body of Christ," (Eph. 4:12). Spiritual gifts are to be used to build up the body of Christ, not to tear it down. We labor in the church so we can serve Christ more effectively. We use our gift to build up the body of Christ so that we might do the work of ministry. Both in his letter to the Ephesians and to the Corinthians, Paul stresses the importance of edification. In Ephesians 4:14-16, Paul confronts the immaturity of those who cause disunity in the Church.

Immaturity in the Church

Paul devoted much of his writing to the problem of divisiveness in the church. Many of his epistles focused on the immaturity of Christians who were so intent on getting their own way that they caused strife and division in the church. He encouraged the church to work for unity by reaching toward the "full maturity of Christ." In the fourteenth verse of Ephesians 4, Paul drew upon the image first of an immature child to warn his readers about their behavior. Then he changed his metaphor to a ship that was caught on waves without a rudder. He turned again to another metaphor of dice in a game used by one who misled and cheated his victims. The mature Christian is founded on Christ, the solid foundation. He or she will "reach toward maturity." The Church that is built on the foundation of Christ can withstand all kinds of doctrinal differences, because its central creed is "Christ is Lord". The church will continuously labor to be a united church within, and then it will seek to be more united without.

The Pastor as Enabler

In striving to invoke the gifts of the believers, the pastor is to be the enabler to try to help build up the body of Christ. The pastor is not to do all the work of the church, but help equip others to do this work. The Dean of the School of Music cannot lead all of the music in our churches across our country. He helps train others so there might be more ministers of music in our churches. The dean of a medical school will not practice all the medicine done in all the states. He trains others to practice medicine. The dean of a law school does not do all of the legal work across our state. She helps prepare others in law so they might do the necessary legal work. A part of the function of a pastor and other staff members is to help train and equip other people to work to do ministry. We make a mistake when we think all we do is hire other people to do ministry for us. The church calls all of us to engage in ministry.

Our Ministry in the World

What is the work of ministry? Micah reminds us that our ministry is in the world, to do justice, to love mercy, and to walk humbly with our God. Paul writes in II Corinthians 5:18 that we have "the ministry of reconciliation." In this ministry of reconciliation, we are charged to bring persons into a vital relationship with God when they have been separated by sin. We are also charged to reach out and bring people together who have been alienated from each other. We have the ministry of reconciliation, not one of dividing the church, but to seek to restore relationships between individuals when they are broken so we can all serve God more effectively.

Personal Ministry

Paul uses a phrase in Romans 2:16 and 2 Timothy 2:8 where he writes "according to 'my' gospel." You might want to say, "Wait a minute, Paul. 'My' gospel. Isn't it 'the' gospel?" Yes, it is "the" gospel, but the gospel becomes most effective when it becomes "my" gospel and "your" gospel when we share our experience with Christ. We have all heard someone ask: "I wonder what can help me get over this particular physical problem I have." People may offer you all kinds of suggestions. Then somebody says, "Well, let me tell you what cured me..." That is a whole different insight. You don't hear them merely philosophizing or guessing about a cure, you hear somebody say what made a radical difference in his or her life. When you and I have experienced the power of Christ and had our gifts evoked, then we are to go into the world and give our lives in service for him.

In Connecticut there is a state law which says that all church doors have to open outwardly. I think that is a good spiritual law as well. After we have gathered together for worship, then the doors ought to open outwardly so that we can go into the world to minister for our Lord. Remember we are not to spend all of our time staying inside a church building. We are to carry our gifts of ministry into the world to glorify God.

Here are the words from I Peter 4:10-11: "As each has received a gift, employ it for one another, as good stewards of God's varied grace: whoever speaks, as one who utters oracles of God; whoever renders service, as one who renders it by the strength by God's supplies; in order that in everything God may be glorified through Jesus Christ. To him belongs glory and dominion forever and ever."

Let everything we do be to glorify God, to build up the body of Christ and to equip ourselves for ministry in the world. Discover your gifts and having discovered them, use them then for God's glory.

[2] Karl Barth, Files of Commission I, World Council of Churches, Geneva, first draft of Barth's article for *The Universal Church in God's Design*, quoted in *The Realm of Redemption* by J. Robert Nelson (Greenwich: The Seabury Press, 1951), 145.

5.
How Are We Going to Support the Church?
The Importance of Stewardship

A visitor dropped in on a church one Sunday in which they were having a special stewardship drive. When the ushers passed the offering plate, he dropped in a bill from his pocketbook. When they passed the offering plate the second time, he dropped in several fifty-cent pieces and quarters. Then, when they passed it the third time, he dropped in the rest of the change from his pocket. As the ushers prepared to pass the offering plate the fourth time, the woman sitting next to him expressed his feelings: "What are they going to do now, search us?" Where are you in your spiritual relationship regarding your money and God? This is a very important area of life. Jesus did not blink at dealing with this relationship. In fact, more of his parables focus on stewardship than any other topic.

Spiritualize the Material

Begin by reflecting on the necessity of spiritualizing the material. In Psalm 24: 1-10, the psalmist reminds us that the earth is the Lord's—all of it—not just what happens in the sanctuary. But the earth is the Lord's. Notice the verb that the psalmist uses. It is not "was," or "will be," but "the earth is the Lord's"—all of it.

Years ago, when I was a child, I used to watch old Western movies built around the theme of claim jumpers. Miners would make a big discovery and rush to the claim office and try to stake their claim before somebody else could beat them to it. Sometimes a claim jumper would rush to the claim office ahead of the real owner and try to take over somebody else's claim. I always knew what would happen. There would be a big shootout at the end of the movie. Since Adam and Eve, there have been a lot of claim jumpers in the world. The socialists claim that the earth belongs to the state. The communists say it belongs to the workers. The capitalists say that it belongs to those who have the initiative to acquire and preserve it. But they are all wrong. The earth is the Lord's. We do not own any of it. We are only stewards of the earth.

That message seems to be belied on almost every hand today. Tractor-trailer trucks roll down the highway with the name of its owner printed on its side. Retail stores flash with the name of its individual firm. Television, radio, computers, billboards, newspapers and magazines tell us about other owners of the earth. Everywhere we look, we see all kinds of indications that somebody else owns the earth. But we do not understand the reality of creation if we see ourselves as masters of the earth. The psalmist asserts that the earth is the Lord's, and we are only stewards of it. God has given his created world to us as a gift, and we can use and develop it. But we do not own it nor possess it.

God Created a Universe

In the ancient Greek thinking, the body was seen as evil. They believed that one should escape the flesh. But the Jewish-Christian tradition has always taught that the body is good. It was created by God, and the body is the temple of the Holy Spirit where God continues to rule and reign. The world which God created is called a universe—not a multi-verse. It is a universe, united by God who created his world with cohesiveness, oneness, and inter-relatedness. At the center of the universe is a spiritual force—God's presence. God's power unifies all of creation and life. God created a universe. Too often we try to divide life into the sacred and the secular, and the two are never supposed to meet. What a person does in church does not touch his or her life outside church. Religion is one thing, but the work-a-day world is seen as something else altogether. Jesus never made that kind of division between the sacred and secular. They are intertwined. What one does in his or her work and the rest of life is a reflection of one's religion.

Back in the Middle Ages, there was a man named Simeon Stylites who for thirty years lived on a platform thirty feet off the ground. People sent his food and every necessity up to him. For thirty years, he never came down from that platform. He was separating himself from the world seeking to follow the injunction of Jesus "to be separate from the world." But that was not the kind of separation for which Jesus was calling. That's foolishness. To separate oneself from the world like that prevents them from being the salt, the light, or the leaven. We are to be separated from evil, but the Christian is called to be the transforming, redemptive force to change society.

A Word from Jesus about Ownership

Notice what Jesus said about ownership. In Matthew 6: 19-24, Jesus cautioned persons about the danger of seeing their clothing as a sign of permanent wealth. Jesus warned that moths might easily destroy the wealth tied up in clothes. Others thought that they could have great possessions by putting their money in grain. The word "rust" is really better translated "eaten away." Mice or rats might enter a granary and destroy the grain. Others put their trust for security in gold. Unfortunately, gold could be easily stolen. Many ancient houses were made of mud, and one could simply knock a hole through the wall or dig through it and steal somebody's gold. Jesus said: "Do not put your ultimate trust in clothes that will wear out, in possessions that can be eroded away, or in money that can be stolen. The failure of many prominent financial institutions and the large decline in the stock market remind us today about putting too much trust in material things. Put your trust in something that will last—something that has eternal significance." The Scriptures do not say that money is the root of all evil. It says that "*the love of money* is the root of all evil."

Money can be used for spiritual ends. It can be spiritualized and used in God's kingdom. When we begin to see that the earth is the Lord's and everything that we have belongs to him, then, we realize that all we have can be used in ways to further his kingdom. We have to learn, first of all, to spiritualize the material. This means that everything we have—our houses, lands, automobiles, bank accounts—all belong to the Lord, and we are simply stewards of it. We use what God has given us. We spiritualize the material when we use the material for spiritual ends. The way we use our possessions testifies to the deeper values in our lives.

Materialize the Spiritual

Secondly, we have got to materialize the spiritual. There are some "holy folks" who just love to talk about how spiritual they are. They claim that they are more spiritual than we are because of the way they pray, or because they have received a "special blessing" or something else. But the sad thing is that their spirituality is often in some lofty, high ideals. It never touches life. You can't get a handle on it. In fact, you can't even see it in their lives. What they say is not reflected in what they do. They talk about religion, but they do not live it. They sometimes even pray about religion, but their lives do not reflect it in any way. Religion is some lofty ideal. Church to them is cloudy and vague but never takes on reality. Church is always more than place, but it is a place. Church doesn't just exist as an idea. Jesus established his church as a living, functioning organism. Religion, if it is real, has always got to have a material reflection.

A Processional Psalm

Psalm 24 is called a processional psalm. Pilgrims were traveling to Jerusalem to worship God in their holy Temple. As they approached the city gates, they cried out: "Lift up the gates." Response came from the priest inside or a chorus who asked the pilgrims: "Who can ascent to the hill of the Lord?" The response came from another choir or priest who declared: "Those who have clean hands and pure hearts." Do you hear it? Religion is reflected in material life. It is not enough just to come inside the temple. Those who came to worship in the temple were expected to let their religion be seen in their living, in their relationships with one another, and in their business dealings. This was symbolized in their clean hands. As Micah declared: "What does the Lord require of you but to do justice, to love mercy, and to walk humbly with your God?" (Micah 6:8) Those who claim that religion takes place only inside of church buildings have never understood the message of the Bible. Religion touches all of life.

This was illustrated for me superbly a number of years ago when I came across a Peanut's comic strip. Snoopy is sitting in the snow shivering. Charlie Brown and Linus see him in that sad condition. "You know, we should do something about that," Linus says. "He looks cold and hungry. Let's go over and help him." So he walks over and pats him on the head and says, "Be warmed, be fed, be comforted." Then he walks off and leaves him shivering in the cold.

That story is straight out of the New Testament where James declares that faith without works is dead (James 2: 17). It is easy to talk about how much I love God, how I love religion, or even to sing pious songs, chant pious prayers, or preach lofty sermons. We can sit and look so pious, but if our religion doesn't touch our living, it is nonsense and not real at all. Faith without works is dead.

God Created the Material World

God was not ashamed of the material world. He created it from nothing. God created material things, including man and woman, and said of all his creation: "It is good."—not perfect—but good. When God became incarnate, he came into the world in the flesh. He entered the world as a human being and dwelt among us. William Temple, a noted English theologian, once said that Christianity is "the most avowedly materialistic of all the great religions." Why would a theologian make such a claim? Because God created the material world. Because the Word became flesh. God did not view flesh or the world as evil, nor did he see material things as evil. The material is a means of grace. Jesus was often seen eating in the homes of wealthy persons. But what did he do when he was there? He challenged them to use their wealth for higher spiritual needs, never to make money as an end in itself.

The Importance of the Tithe

I believe that one of the biblical injunctions which enables us to get outside of ourselves and to commit ourselves to God's way is through the giving of our tithe. A tithe is one-tenth of your income. I learned about tithing as a young man and since that time I have tithed. My wife and I have tithed in every church where we have served. This is not about legalism. We have searched our hearts and have always sought to do what we felt would enable us to support God's work and try to get beyond our own selfish concerns. The dedication of a part of our income is a way of seeking to make the whole spiritual. I am convinced that if more people tithed, our church would certainly not have any financial problems at all.

A small girl was turning the pages in a book and marking words she didn't know. She passed over the big word stewardship, and her mother stopped her and asked: "Now honey, do you know the meaning of that word?" She looked up at her mother and said, "It means that we may have money, but we are supposed to use it to help others." That was very incisive for a young girl. We may have great possessions, but they are not supposed to be used selfishly for our own ends. All of our possessions are to be used in service for the God we worship.

Updating Our Giving

If a church had 340 families that made at least $30,000 a year and they tithed, their church would receive more than a million dollars in gifts. If we had

200 families that made at least $50,000 a year and they tithed, we would receive more than a million dollars. Do you see what I am saying? Few of the people in most churches tithe and this is the challenge before our churches. Now I know that we have some elderly people who are on a fixed income from social security. But many of these people give very faithfully and in a dedicated way to the church. My prayer is that all of us will seek to be faithful in what we give to our church. We all know that these are difficult times but the ministries of the church continue just as our personal needs do. Every single person's gift and tithe is important and essential. If every person honored his or her pledge to our churches, every church could reach its budget and financial goals without any difficulty.

James Denney, the Scottish theologian, once said: "I would like to stand in front of every church and lift up a crucifix and declare: 'He did this for you. Christ died for you and me.'" Having received so much from Christ, how can we take it all for granted without making a commitment to him? Our stewardship arises out of our acknowledgment of God as creator, out of an acknowledgment of Christ as redeemer, and commitment to him and his Church as the agent of reconciliation.

Some of us, however, are still giving to our church like we may have done thirty years ago. Let's draw an illustration from the tooth fairy. The columnist, Eric Zorn of *The Chicago Tribune*, drew on the U. S. Department of Labor's consumer price index to see if the tooth fairy is given more or less these days compared to say thirty years ago. Some parents complain today that now they put a dollar under their child's pillow when they only got a quarter as a child. They say their child is getting so much more. Zorn, with calculator in hand, said that if a child got a quarter in 1970 and in 2008 he gets a dollar, it is not more but less. The dollar of today is the equivalent of about ten cents in 1964. In 1946 when a person put a dollar in the collection plate that may have seemed like a generous gift. But that 1946 dollar today is the equivalent of five cents or less. Anyone who goes to the grocery store and buys grocery or buys anything today knows what inflation has done. The average income in 1970 was $17,550. The average house in 1970 costs $58,500, and a gallon of gas was 88 cents.

Many of these same people, however, when they come to church seem to forget about inflation. They want to put the same thing in the collection plate that they put in thirty years ago or ten years ago. A dollar that was placed in the offering plate in 1970 would need to have at least five dollars in the offering plate today to be equal. Or if one put five dollars in the offering plate in 1970, then you would need to have $25 today. Or if you put $25 in 1970, it would probably have to be at least $125 today to be on the same level. We cannot give today as we did ten years, five years or especially twenty years ago and think we are giving the same kind of gifts. We need to increase our giving if our giving is even going to be on the same level to what it used to be.

Yes, it is challenging to give to support our budget today and to all of our mission causes. But it would not be a challenge if every single person tithed or gave faithfully. Instead of leaving it to a few to carry the whole load, if each of us shared the load, it would be much easier to bear. Spiritual feelings are not enough. There have to be materialistic ends. Our goals and desires must be fulfilled in action and tithes. Jesus says that where your treasure is there will be your heart. If our heart is in the right place, the treasures—tithes and offerings—that come from our hands will represent our love for God and our concern for others.

I heard Grady Nutt, who was a Baptist minister, a humorous and at one time a regular on the old Hee Haw show on television and was unfortunately killed in a plane crash several years ago, pray a prayer that included the following lines: "Lord, we know you love a cheerful giver but I believe that you also love a grumpy giver as well, because you love all of us." Whether you give from the most positive motives or from some other persuasion, your church needs your support and you need the spiritual discipline of giving and spiritualizing the whole of your material possessions.

The Offering at the End of the Service

James Cleland, who was Dean of the Chapel at the Duke Divinity School several years ago, asked a group of ministers at a conference what was the high point of the worship service for them. Most of the ministers said the sermon. Some said the music. One even said the benediction, which may have reflected his delight that the service was over. If the minister dared to ask the congregation, many might say that was the high point for them. But for a minister that is kind of surprising. But Dr. Cleland indicated that he thought that the high point of the worship service was the offering. The offering according to him, should come at the end of the service. The offering is our response to the preaching of the Word and a symbolic way of giving ourselves.

Having the offering taken at the end of the service denotes that our gifts are in response to the total proclamation of the word of God through music, preaching, praying, and everything else that had happened in the experience of worship. Our giving is a reflection of our own gratitude to God. In pledging to support the church budget, you have an opportunity to get the priorities right in your own life. By giving a portion of your income to the church, you seek to spiritualize the whole of your material resources. Give from the first fruits of your life that you might magnify God.

Years ago when highwaymen would attempt to rob someone, they would cry: "Your money or your life. Everyone, of course, would give up his money rather than his life. Jesus said, "I have come that you might have life"—not money. Money is a way of serving him in all that we do and have. Money is not the end goal of our living, but a means of enabling us to share the "life" which we have found in God.

During WWII, an officer challenged his soldiers to go on a very dangerous mission. "I could appoint three men to go on this mission," he said, "but I would like three volunteers. I'm going to turn my back," he declared, "and see if three volunteers will step forward." He turned his back and waited a moment, then, when he turned around he could not see any difference in the troops. No one seemed to step forward. He looked rather irritated and was about to speak when his sergeant spoke up and said: "But, sir, the whole battalion has stepped forward—all of us have stepped forward."

The church has a great challenge before us. I hope that every single one of you will step forward and do your part and bear the stewardship responsibility of our church. The earth is the Lord's and all that we have belongs to him. Let us be faithful in our stewardship. It is time for each of us to step forward.

6.
WHAT'S OUR BUSINESS OUTSIDE THIS BUILDING?
THE CHURCH'S MISSION

Several years ago I heard a parable which I have not forgotten. On one of the coasts of our country some lifeguards were charged with the responsibility of protecting the lives of the swimmers along that section of the beach. The lifeguards would launch their boats and row out when the waves were high and treacherous to save people when they were drowning. These lifeguards were very efficient. No waves were ever too high, no difficulty too great for them. One day they rescued a man from drowning, and this man was so grateful that he wanted to do something for the lifeguards. He decided to build a beautiful lifeguard station on the shore. It was a first class building. It was air-conditioned and had all the comforts they could possibly want. It had a kitchen, den area with a television and comfortable beds. Soon the lifeguards spent more and more of their time in the beautiful house on the beach. People could be screaming for help in the water, but the lifeguards did not hear their cries because they were inside enjoying all the comforts of the lifeguard station.

To me this is a parable about the church. You think about it for a moment. The church was established to reach out and bring the message of salvation to those who do not know Jesus Christ as Lord. Often we build beautiful buildings, as we have done. Religious people gather inside their beautiful buildings and enjoy the comfort and convenience but forget that they have been commissioned to go outside these buildings and reach persons who do not know Christ.

Matthew 28: 19-20 points this out very vividly. The disciples of Jesus had gathered on some unknown mountain to meet him after the resurrection. We do not know which mountain, but it was someplace in Galilee. Matthew does not mention the resurrection appearances of Jesus in Jerusalem. Suddenly Jesus appeared to the disciples. Paul writes that Jesus appeared to over five hundred people who had gathered there (1 Cor. 15:6). In that appearance, Jesus gave his disciples what you and I usually call the Great Commission (Matthew 28: 19-20). He charged his followers with their missionary responsibility. Look with me at the message Jesus gave them.

Claim of Great Authority

First, Jesus made a claim of great authority. He says, "All authority on heaven and earth has been given to me." What a tremendous claim! And this claim is echoed through the New Testament. You find this theme in many of Paul's epistles. I mention only two examples. Paul writes that the glorified Christ when raised from the dead was seated at the right hand of the Father and "is far above all rule and authority and power and dominion, and above every name that is named, not only in this age but also in that which is to come; and he has put all things under his feet" (Eph. 1:20-21). In another place Paul writes: "Therefore God has highly exalted him and bestowed on him the name which is above every name, that at the name of Jesus every knee should bow, in heaven and on earth and under the earth, and every tongue confess that Jesus Christ is Lord, to the glory of God the Father" (Phil. 2:7-11). We can find other references in I Peter 1:21 and also in Hebrews 2:9. In the Book of Revelation, John states: "Worthy is the Lamb who was slain, to receive power and wisdom and might and honor and glory and blessing" (Rev. 5:12).

There is no question that the New Testament ascribes to Jesus Christ all authority. The interesting thing is that down through the ages since the coming of Jesus, persons have found that Jesus does make a tremendous claim on their lives. Kings, presidents, emperors, peasants, wealthy and poor persons, scholars and illiterates, poets, musicians, artists, scientists have all felt the tremendous claim of Jesus Christ. Lives have been transformed by this allegiance. "All authority," Jesus claims, "is mine." We, as Christians, gather in this place to worship and also acknowledge that we stand under his authority. He is Lord of our lives. We, too, acknowledge Christ's claim of authority on our own lives.

An Announcement of Jesus' Commission

Secondly, we notice in this passage that Jesus gave the church an announcement of his commission. It is a shame that we do not have a verb in English for "disciple," because the key emphasis in verse nineteen is "make disciples." "As you are going," "as you are baptizing," "as you are teaching," are all subordinate to "make disciples." All of these verbs are participles. The imperative in Greek is "make disciples." We are charged to "make disciples."

We Assume Most Are Already Christians

How do the followers of Jesus make disciples? Jesus begins by saying, "As you are going." Jesus is assuming that anyone who is his disciple is going to share the good news of salvation with others. Why don't we go? Well, I think, for one thing, we assume that most everybody around us is already Christian. In surveys that have been taken in our country, almost everybody acknowledges that this is a Christian country. They have a naive assumption that in some way most people are already Christians. Many believe that being born in America in some hocus-pocus fashion makes them a Christian. George Gallop, Jr., several years ago did a survey in which a majority of Americans consider themselves to be Christians. He summarized his conclusion this way.

We boast Christianity as our faith, but many of us have not bothered to learn the basic biblical facts of this religion. Many of us dutifully attend church, but this act appears to have made us no less likely than any unchurched brethren to engage in unethical behavior.

We say we are Christians, but sometimes we do not show much love toward those who do not share our particular religious perspective. We say we rejoice in the good news that Jesus brought, but we are often strangely reluctant to share the gospel with others. In a typical day the average person stays in front of the T.V. set nearly 25 times longer than in prayer. We say we are believers, but perhaps we are only assenters.[1]

Maybe that is the reason evangelists like Billy Graham and others have said that the greatest mission field today may be inside the church and not outside. Some of those on the church rolls have been inoculated with a mild dose of Christianity and this has made them immune to the real thing. We often don't share the message with others because we assume that everybody is Christian and does not need the gospel.

You likely have heard the story about the preacher and one of his laymen who went to visit some homes in the neighborhood of the church. As they pulled up in front of the house they were going to visit, they saw two Cadillacs and a Mercedes in the driveway, along with a big boat. They walked toward the door and saw the man sitting in front of his huge television set drinking a can of beer as he watched a ball game. The layman looked over at the preacher and asked, "What good news do we have to share with this man?"

That is where we are in our modern society today, isn't it? If a person is wealthy, healthy and wise, many feel we have no good news for them. We assume that these people are Christians. We know nothing about the brokenness, fragmentation, and lost condition in their lives. We assume these people are Christians, when they may be without purpose, meaning, forgiveness, hope and love. Many long for wholeness and faith. We have a word they need to hear.

We Are Timid

Sometimes we are really afraid to talk to others. We would like to, but are really timid about taking that step. I know this feeling. As a young Minister, I would sometimes go visit somebody who was supposed to be a prospect for our church, who was not Christian, and I knew I had to talk with them. I would knock on the door and sometimes I would pray silently to myself: "Oh, Lord, don't let them be at home." We all have those kinds of feelings of timidity at times.

Embarrassed by Some Evangelism Methods

Sometimes we do not share the good news with others because we are embarrassed by some of the approaches which some evangelists have used. We are uncomfortable with some preacher standing in a person's face shaking a Bible, grabbing them by the lapel, or using some gosh-awful pious language and images that we don't like. We often refuse to do anything, because we don't want to be associated with these negative ways.

Don't Know What to Say

Sometimes we don't share the good news because we just don't know what to say. We really feel like we haven't been trained. Several years ago, I have done training programs in former churches where I have been pastor or interim pastor to help equip people to share the good news more effectively. All Christians need to be trained.

Why Share the Gospel?

The Command of Our Lord

Why should we share the good news of Jesus Christ with others? First, it is the command of Christ to share the good news. In Matthew's Gospel Jesus commanded us to make disciples. Jesus called his disciples to be fishers of men and women. Jesus, said, "You are to be my witnesses." In 2 Corinthians 5: 18-20, we are reminded that we are to be "ambassadors for Christ." You and I are called to tell others about Christ. Evangelism/missions are the responsibility of every Christian, not just the pastor and staff. The church would have died out a long time ago if only the professional clergy were charged to witness to the faith. If you are a Christian, you share the responsibility of bearing the good news of Christ to other persons. Every Christian is an evangelist.

Oh, I love the story about the woman who came back into her house after talking to a man who had knocked on the door. After she left, her husband asked, "What did he want?" "Oh, he wanted to know if I were Christian," the wife said. "Why didn't you tell him it was none of his business?" the husband replied. "If you had heard him talk," the wife answered, "you would have thought it was his business." Evangelism/missions are your business and mine. It is the business of all Christians to share the good news of Christ with others.

Our Concern for Others

Why do we want to share the good news of Christ with other people? A second reason is our sense of concern for others who have not heard the saving knowledge of Christ. If you and I have experienced the forgiving grace of God, why would we not want to share this wonderful news with others, who also need to have that experience of forgiveness and grace? Would we not want to share this message out of a sense of the love and joy which we have experienced from Christ? Having experienced God's abundant love, surely we will want to tell others about that love.

Suppose I had found a cure for cancer and you were in the hospital dying with cancer and I came to see you. Suppose I came into your room and fluffed up your pillow and talked to you about the UNC, NC State, Wake Forest, UVA or VA Tech football games. Suppose I continued to talk with you about the weather, our mutual friends, or other matters, but never shared my cure for cancer with you. What would you think? We are charged with a mission to bear the good news of Christ with others—"as you are going make disciples." At the CBF national meeting in Memphis, Tennessee, we heard from numerous persons who are serving as CBF missionaries around the world and in our own country. These are persons who are committed to sharing the Good News "as they are going."

As You Are Baptizing

But also Jesus said, "As you are baptizing, make disciples." We are baptizing persons who have committed their lives to Christ. Baptism is a dramatic parable about the radical change in a person's life. In the early church, we see numerous ways the disciples witnessed for Christ. One way was through preaching and teaching. They often started preaching in the synagogues and when they could no longer do that, they would preach on street corners or any place people would listen. They also would bear personal witness to Christ. When Andrew met Jesus, he went immediately and told Simon Peter, his brother, about Jesus. When Philip met Jesus, he in turn told Nathaniel. The disciples were busy telling others about Jesus. They also went from one house to another sharing the news about Jesus Christ. Sometimes a church service was held in somebody's house (Acts 20:20; 10:27-28; 16:15). The disciples likewise shared out of their own personal experience their story about what Christ had done for them. That which they had seen and heard, they told about (I John 1:1-3). Paul continuously told his conversion story (Acts 22:1-21). Later the disciples would share through literary means—the gospels—their witness to Christ. Paul wrote many letters to bear witness to the faith. We all can witness in a variety of ways.

In What Way Did They Share the Faith?

How did they share their faith? They shared

the gospel wherever they met people and with whatever opportunities they had. Paul and Peter spoke in the synagogues. They spoke about Christ in the home of Cornelius or at the gate of the temple. They witnessed to Christ in a jail, in the marketplace, on Mars Hill in Athens, on the roadside or in a home. They utilized any occasion they had.

How, did they share the gospel? They did it with enthusiasm. They spoke with so much enthusiasm that one time they were accused of being drunk (Acts 2:13). You recall the story in Acts. The disciples were excited about what God had done in Jesus Christ and were filled with the Spirit. The disciples also were courageous in their witness. Stephen was stoned as he bore witness to Christ. Paul suffered much persecution to carry the message of Christ to others. The disciples also drew on the Scriptures as their source of authority. They frequently quoted from the Old Testament to show how it pointed to Jesus as the Messiah. They always pointed men and women to Jesus Christ and the difference he could make in their lives.

Alexander Whyte was a noted preacher at St. George's Church in Edinburgh. One day a man came by to see him. On Sunday he had invited a friend to come to church with him. Rigby, a commercial traveler, often visited Edinburgh on business. He would stay at a local hotel. He always invited some stranger to come with him to church. The man he invited on Sunday at first refused but later at Rigby's persistence came with him. The man was so overtaken by Whyte's preaching that he came back that night and silently made a commitment of faith to Jesus Christ. Rigby shared that news with Mr. Whyte.

"God bless you for telling me," Whyte said. "I thought Sunday night's sermon fell flat and I was very depressed about it." And then Whyte said: "I didn't quite catch your name." 'Rigby,' the man said. 'Rigby," responded Whyte, "I have been looking for you for years." He ran back into his study and came out with a huge stack of letters. He told him that he had letters from numerous men who told him about being invited to church by a man named Rigby. In his bundle of letters, twelve came from young men, four of whom had committed their lives to the ministry. All of this came about because one man invited others to church. Like this man, whatever opportunities you and I have, we need to use them to point others to Christ.

As You Teach

"Make disciples as you teach," Jesus said. One of the primary ministries of the church is to teach. Our purpose is to make disciples not just converts. Converts need to become disciples. Converts need to grow in their knowledge of the faith. We have too many people who are still right where they were when they became a Christian. They haven't grown. They are still baby Christians. We see this all the time in the church.

I have talked to a number of ministers over the years who say that one of the criticisms they often hear is: "We are leaving, because we are not being fed." What the ministers have discovered is that these people are upset because they are not being fed what they want to hear. They want religious pabulum. Many want sermons to focus on how to be converted. That theme, they think, doesn't touch them. They have already heard that. William H. Hinson, senior pastor of First United Methodist Church in Houston, Texas, observed: Oftentimes I have felt like saying to such persons, "Why don't you take the cross off the altar and replace it with a feeding trough? If your only concern is to fill your own spiritual bellies, and if you have no concern for the issues that tear our world apart, why not remove the cross from the altar?"[2]

What is Hinson saying? I think he means that there is a genuine concern to be fed that one might grow and deepen in his or her knowledge of the Christian faith. But some people want to continue to be breast-fed Christians. They want only the milk and not the meat of the word. Their focus in religion is often only as self-interest and what religion can do for them. They are upset at the hard sayings and demands of Jesus, and Paul's writings remain very difficult for them to comprehend. They want the candy, apples, and the sweetness of the faith, but they don't want to deal with the cross and its call for sacrifice and self-sacrificing commitment. Taking up the cross, however, is a radical part of what it means to follow Jesus Christ. It is tragic for someone to enter the doorway of conversion and stop at the entrance and refuse to continue growing.

I am thankful that when I made my commitment to Jesus Christ as Lord I had ministers, teachers and friends who would not let me rest on my spiritual oars but challenged me to think and grow in the faith. They helped me to see what Jesus Christ has come to challenge me to be and become. We should never settle for clichés and slogans about our faith. Jesus Christ wants to pull us forward to wrestle with the toughest questions of life. Baptizing people is not the end but the beginning of a lifetime of learning about Christ and his way. One of the primary obligations of the pulpit and the church is to teach Christians how to grow in the faith. We are challenged to spend a life time learning about the life, death, resurrection and teachings of Jesus. Paul's teachings, the great doctrines of the faith and the meaning and witness of the Church are a part of the knowledge we seek to understand.

Evangelism Is Not Limited to Words

Evangelism is not limited to speaking about Christ. Sometimes the most effective way to reach someone for Christ is to meet a personal need in their life. It is hard to speak to someone about Christ when they are dying from hunger or have some other physical need. We may need first to give them food or meet some other need in their lives before we talk to them. A cup of cold water or some clothing may open a closed door. If we try only words and refuse to put action to our words, then we may leave the beggar at the gate, the woman at the well, the blind in their darkness, the deaf in their soundless world, the lame in their paralysis, the hungry in their want, the poor in their poverty, the hopeless in their despondency, the inmates in their prison, or the hurting man or woman beside their road. Meeting human need and confronting genuine needs are an essential means of evangelism and missions. Both words and actions are needed for genuine evangelism. Words are seldom enough. James reminds us, "So with faith; if it does not lead to action, it is in itself a lifeless thing" (James 2: 17 New English Bible).

A Continuous Presence

Finally, Jesus gives us assurance of a continuous presence. First, Jesus assures us of a personal presence. "I am with you always." "I am." "I am" echoes throughout the Gospel of John. "I am the Bread of Life.' "I am Light of the world." "I am the true vine." "I am the resurrection." "I am with you always." But Jesus states that he is also an abiding presence. "I am with you always." Jesus Christ, through the power of the Holy Spirit, is always with us no matter what the circumstances of life might be. When we seek to bear witness to our faith, Jesus Christ, through God's Spirit, is there helping us make that witness. Jesus is also the triumphant presence. "I am with you until the end of the ages." History will not come to an end with a whimper without direction and guidance. However history ends, we know that God is in control of history.

We can be thankful that we can gather together and be in a place where we have an opportunity to learn and grow spiritually. But we need to remember that our major mission, after we have worshiped together, is to go into the world and share the good news of Jesus Christ with other persons.

During the Second World War when Helmut Thielicke was pastor in Stuttgart, Germany, the allied forces were bombing the city severely. One night a group of men had descended into a cellar for protection from the falling bombs. The next morning when Pastor Thielicke arrived on the scene, there was a gaping hole where the cellar had been. A woman came over to the minister and asked, "Are you Pastor Thielicke?" When he said he was, she said, "My husband was down there last night (as she pointed to the hole). All they found of him was his cap. We heard you preach. I want to thank you for getting him ready for eternity."

We are all preparing for eternity. God give us the courage and the joy to share the good news of Christ which we have experienced so that all persons will know it.

[1]George Gallup, Jr. and George O'Connell, *What Do Americans Say that I AM* (Philadelphia: Westminster, 1986), 88-89.

[2]William H. Hinson, *A Place to Dig In* (Nashville: Abingdon Press, 1987), 20.

7.

DOES ANYBODY REALLY CARE?
THE FELLOWSHIP OF THE CHURCH

Sometime ago I sat across the table at lunch with a fellow pastor. He looked over at me and asked: "Does what happens in church make any real difference in the lives of any of our church members?" He was at a low moment in his life, because his church was divided with all kinds of factions. He had seen the church at its worst and had little faith at the moment that it could be different. Anyone who has been in church work long understands that feeling.

The New Testament, however, gives us a high concept of what the church ought to be. Those of us who are members of the church have a high concept of what the church ought to be, but sometimes, instead of church members meeting that high ideal, we see that some churches are often filled with conflicts, power struggles, factions, assertive behavior, ego trips, or those who want to have their way regardless of the opinions of others. There are thousands on church rolls, yet when the church gathers together, there is often only a handful of people that meet. An announcement can be made in a church service on

Sunday morning such as, "We will gather together on Wednesday night for our church supper or for our monthly church conference," but that gathering is often a very small handful. In most of our churches only a few of the members are really involved. Most are on the fringes.

The Term Fellowship

The word fellowship is an important New Testament word. To many persons in church today, however, the word fellowship usually means a get-together for the young people or adults in some kind of social context such as a picnic, a luncheon, a meal of some kind where cookies and punch are served. That is the concept of the fellowship of the church which too many church members have.

The New Testament word fellowship or communion comes from the Greek word *Koinonia* which is used eighteen times in the New Testament. *Koinonia* is a far broader word than a description for social relationships. It is a word that depicts a unique relationship of the Christian with God and with fellow Christians. It was said of the early disciples that "they devoted themselves to the apostles' teachings and to the fellowship" (Acts 2:42). There are some who have said that this relationship of the early disciples was so unique because it was conditioned by their special relationship with the risen Christ and the apostles that it is unrepeatable today. If that is the case, then we are in deep trouble indeed as churches today. The German theologian, Dietrich Bonhoeffer, however, challenges that view. "The first disciples lived in the bodily presence and communion of Jesus...So far from impoverishing them his departure brings a new gift. The disciples enjoyed exactly the same bodily communion as is available for us today, nay rather, our communion with him is richer and more assured than it was for them, for the communion and presence which we have is that of the glorified Lord."[1] Bonhoeffer reminds us that we ought to have an even greater sense of our relationship to God in the fellowship of the church today than the early disciples because of the presence of the risen Lord with his church.

I want us to reflect on this fellowship of togetherness called church, this special community of commitment and faith, this fellowship with a difference. Let us look at this unique relationship that we are supposed to have with God through the fellowship of the church. I want us to examine this fellowship under four headings.

The Fellowship of the Redeemed

First, there is the fellowship of the redeemed. Paul, writing to the Corinthian church, observed: "God is faithful by whom you were called into the fellowship of his Son, Jesus Christ our Lord" (I Cor. 1:9). We enter this fellowship by a very personal relationship with the redeeming Lord Jesus Christ. The church advertises itself as a "fellowship of sinners." We are sinners saved by grace, but sinners still.

An Exclusive Fellowship

The church then has an exclusive membership. It is a membership made up only of those who have committed their lives to Christ as Lord. Membership in the fellowship begins with a confession of faith that Jesus Christ is Lord. "They made a complete dedication of themselves first to the Lord" (2 Cor. 8: 8 Phillips). Believers in Christ's Lordship are part of the Christian fellowship. Those who have been baptized upon confession of faith are part of this community of believers. Like John, we testify to that which we have heard and seen (I John 1: 1-3). Those who are unwilling to make this kind of allegiance are excluded from this fellowship. The Lordship of Jesus Christ is an absolute claim. When we say that we make Jesus lord of our lives, this means that he is lord above everything else in our lives, or he should be. We renounce all other claims to first allegiance in our lives.

There are some, of course, who are offended by such statements as these. From the very beginning, however, this kind of claim was an offense to unbelievers. This scandal of the Christian faith could not be accepted by many.

Did you hear about the small boy who told his father that he was tired of going to Sunday School. "Why?" his father asked. "Because all I ever hear is Jesus, Jesus, Jesus." Well, that is what the church is all about, isn't it? Jesus, JESUS! Our mission is to declare the good news about what God has done through Jesus Christ. There are some people who will be offended by that message. But the early disciples were bold to declare that there was "no other name under heaven where we can be saved" (Acts 4:12). Jesus, our Lord, declared, "I am the way, the truth, and the life; no one comes unto the father but by me" (John 14:6). There is an exclusive declaration which the church declares about its membership. The church is a fellowship of the redeemed, those who give their allegiance to Jesus Christ as Lord.

An Inclusive Fellowship

At the same time, the church is also an inclusive fellowship. "Whosoever will may come." Any person, man or woman, regardless of race, can come to know Jesus Christ as Lord. In Jesus Christ there is neither male nor female, slave nor free, Jew nor Greek, educated or uneducated. We are all one in Jesus Christ. All barriers are down. The one time you know for certain that a local church is not Church is when it excludes from its fellowship because of race or sex anyone who wants to confess Jesus Christ as Lord. The ground is level for all persons at the foot of the cross of Jesus Christ. All persons are invited to share in this fellowship. Jesus came that persons might have fellowship with God and other believers. This unique community draws Christians to God and each other. Wherever the Holy Spirit is, there is the Christian community. We begin then with a declaration that we belong to the fellowship of the redeemed, a unique community of those who have committed their lives to Jesus Christ as Lord.

A Fellowship of the Concerned

Secondly, the church is a fellowship of the concerned "Produced a magnificent concern for others" (2Cor. 8:2). Early in its history it was said of the early church, "Behold, how they loved one another." That cannot always be said about our churches today. Nevertheless, where we are genuinely a fellowship of the redeemed, there will be concern. Life teaches us early that caring is a very powerful emotion. Signs on the road remind us, "Pass with care." During World War II persons used to send Care packages. Today we mail a package and have stamped on it, "Handle with care." A husband or wife may ask for some TLC- some "tender loving care." When we are disgusted with something, we sometimes declare, "Well, I couldn't care less!" But that is a sad state to be in, isn't it? We need to care for other people.

Too often we see evidence all around us of a lack of concern. We hear on television or read in the newspaper about individuals who were murdered, raped or robbed and sadly others were standing off at a safe distance, or looking out a window, or standing somewhere nearby or overhearing what is happening and still doing nothing. They don't care. They don't want to get involved. To be uncaring is not only a bad attitude; it may indeed be a great sin. The church should be a community where Christians care for each other, as our Lord cared for all hurting and needy persons who crossed his path-- the poor, blind, deaf, lame, lepers, and the ill. Anyone who had a need, our Lord reached out to touch them with care and affection. The church is to model concern after its Lord.

A Giving Church

A concerned church will be a "giving" church. The Apostle Paul wrote to the Corinthians about their need to support the church in Jerusalem, the mother church (2 Corinthians 8: 1-7). The Jerusalem church was poor and needed some financial assistance. The Corinthian church had said they would send an offering but they had not yet done so. Paul gave them five basic reasons why they ought to help the church in Jerusalem. First, he gave them an example of others who had already helped them. Second, he reminded them of the example of Christ. Then he gave his own example of sacrifice. Next he told them the importance of putting something into action rather than just talking about it. Finally, he emphasized the way life had of repaying kindnesses that are done to others. What Paul was telling them in essence was, "Your deed will be your creed." Your action will demonstrate that you really care for your fellow believers in Jerusalem.

It is awful easy to pass some resolution stating: "We are concerned about the missionaries overseas or we hurt for these starving people." But if we never send a dime or send anybody to assist them, we do not give evidence of real concern. Our personal involvement and our financial support will put our beliefs into practice. We remember the words of James, "Faith without works is dead" (James 2:17).

A Tolerant Church

The church that is a fellowship of concern will also be a church where there is tolerance. A true fellowship can tolerate our differences. Paul writes about the fact that as the body of Christ, the church has many different parts like the human body. In our physical body, we are not all the eye or the ear, the tongue, or the foot, or the nose. Our body is composed of different parts with different functions. So it is with the church. We learn to tolerate or better to affirm these differences, because they are all necessary to carry on the work and ministry of Christ. I have learned a long time ago that the most intolerant people are those who are very insecure themselves. People who have a sense of personal security within their own lives and a sense of their security in their belief about God can tolerate differences in others and do not assume that everyone must think and act like they do. We can live together with differences when we are united in the Lordship of Christ.

Benjamin Garrison made this helpful observation about church. He wrote:

> *Neither is a group of people gathering under a same roof necessarily a church; that is, a household. The group may have activities for the young, projects for the old, and plans for the middle-aged; it may be forward-looking and other-regarding; it may be well-mannered and administered; it may be educational and recreational; the building may even be paid for; it may contain the community's best people who hear the world's best sermons—but still not be a church. What will make it a church is the quality*

of the personal relationships it houses—an openness, an intimacy, a face-to-faceness.[2]

Where there is not a sense of being able to work in a relationship of tolerating differences, our gathering of people is highly unlikely the church. In the community of fellowship there is a concern for each other that reaches out with such love that it embraces all of this community.

A Fellowship of Support

Thirdly, the church will be a fellowship of support. "They simply begged us," Paul wrote, "to accept their gifts and so let them share the honor of supporting their brothers in Christ" (2 Cor. 8: 4 Phillips). This community of faith will support each other in a variety of ways. This kind of support will rarely be discovered merely in the formal occasions when the community of faith gathers together in assembled worship. Worship is essential in the life of a healthy congregation. Personal support is usually found in other ways, however.

The Importance of Small Groups

This support is established mostly in small groups. That is the reason the church has got to have a cluster of small cells where we get to know each other. *Koinonia* comes out of personal participation and mutual sharing in small groups. In these face-to-face meetings, there is give and take. Here intimacy and trust are established. These "cells" feed the living organism called church. Often this is done in Sunday

School classes or small groups or prayer meetings out of the Sunday School or some other organization.

In a congregation where I have served, I have seen several wonderful small groups, like divorce or grief, AIDS, Alzheimer, AA, Bible study or prayer groups which have supported its members in many different ways. They have given clear evidence by their concern for each other that they were a part of the support fellowship of the church. On other occasions, I have seen some people who fell through the cracks and never sensed that support from their small church group. They felt forgotten or ignored. Where the church is truly a fellowship of support, there will be small groups caring for and sustaining each other. *"Koinonia,"* Carlyle Marney said, "is not to have all things in common but to know each other in common."[3] In these small cell groups we really get to know each other, sense the hurt and pain of each other, and can then be supportive and loving. We need these small groups in our churches to express concern in a genuine way.

Bearing the Burdens of Others

Another way of showing support is by bearing each other's burdens. This is where the small group gets underneath another person, when that person is crushed down with grief, illness or some other problem, or their support lets that individual know that the community is there in their time of need, is praying for them, and sustaining them with their presence. They might sometimes bring food, sit with them, stay up with them, help with their children, telephone, run other errands, or do whatever is needed. Here is the real community of support. They know that no one need bear all the pain, hurt or grief alone. They let them know they want to help. As Paul said, "They want to bear one another's burdens" (Gal. 6:2).

In a former church a woman told me that she moved to our city and wanted to find a church where she could be accepted and loved. She started coming to our church, and soon she said the Scripture was truly fulfilled that said, "I was a stranger and you took me in." In our church, she said she found a support group that loved, accepted, and cared for her as a person. That is a marvelous testimony to what we are supposed to be as a fellowship of caring people.

Encourage One Another

We will also be, if we are really supportive of each other, encouraging. We will seek to encourage each other when life is difficult and hard. We will share words of hope and optimism with others, knowing that it is easy to criticize. It is easy to put down another person, but it is much more difficult to lift them up. I urge people to examine their own motive when they want to criticize others. Reflect and think about your own life. What has helped you most? Is it when people have been critical or is it when people have been encouraging?

What builds up the body of Christ? Does criticism or encouragement build up the church? The answer is obvious. Which are you, one who always finds fault with others or someone who seeks to bring solutions to the problems in church?

One of the dear figures in the New Testament is Barnabas. Here also is dedicated Paul who always was the purest. Paul had a high vision of ministry and high expectation of himself and others. But he made a mistake with John Mark. Paul decided not to take John Mark with him on a missionary journey because John Mark had failed him at an earlier point. He had left when the going got tough. But Barnabas said, "I'll take him with me." The church, interestingly enough, prayed for both partners, Paul and Silas and Barnabas and Mark. The church commissioned all four. Paul took Silas with him and Barnabas took John Mark, and they both left with the blessings of the church. Later, Paul wrote to Timothy and told him, "Bring John Mark with you" (II Tim. 4:11). He knew he had been wrong. He recognized his mistake, gave him another chance and encouraged him in his ministry. That ought to be the way of the church. The church fellowship needs to support each other in our highest moments and in our lowest moments. Let's make our genuine care known.

A United Fellowship

Fourth, the church also ought to be a fellowship that is united. This unity is not uniformity. It cannot be and be a real body. But the New Testament stresses the need for unity in the fellowship. This is what happened after Pentecost to the disciples. "They were *all* filled with the Holy Spirit' (Acts 2:4). Peter standing with the eleven said, "We *all* are witnesses" (Acts 2:32). "Grace upon grace came upon them all" (Acts 4:33). They were not isolated serving Christ. After Jesus' ascension, the disciples "with *one* accord devoted *themselves* to prayer" (Acts 1:14). "They were all *together* in one place" (Acts 2:1). After Pentecost, "They attended the temple t*ogether*" (Acts 2:46). "They lifted their voices *together* to God" (Acts 4:24). The whole "company of those who were believers were of *one* heart and of *one* soul" (Acts 4:32). Again and again we read, "They were *all together*" (Acts 5:12). Paul writing to the Corinthian church said, "Just as the body is one and has many members, and all members of the body, though many, are one body, so it is with Christ. For by one spirit we were all baptized into the one body and were all made to drink of one Spirit" (I Cor. 12:12-13). Paul wrote many times about the need for oneness and unity in the church. Divisiveness tears the church apart. He sought to end divisions.

Morton Kelsey wrote an interesting book entitled *Discernment* in which he talked about the struggles in churches that literally distort the fellowship of the church. He is convinced that these kinds of struggles in churches usually activate the demonic. Demonic refers to an evil that invades a situation, group, or individual and takes over the group in ways that are contrary to the well-being of those who are possessed. He makes a distinction between demonic and that which is angelic by saying that the demonic always wants to possess, whereas the angelic, that is, forces representing God's love, wants to relate.[4]

Diversity Not Divisiveness

The church seeks to help people relate to one another and to bring about reconciliation. The church, if it is the church, will not be concerned with making divisions but seeking unity. The church of Jesus Christ which has genuine fellowship will have diversity not divisiveness. It will have cooperation and not competition. It will have differences but not distinctions. It will seek not to be a mob but a movement, not to be isolated individuals but an integrated whole. It will seek not to be a collection of persons but a congregation which works together. It will not be an organization but a living organism which is alive and working to serve Jesus Christ, who is Lord of the Church.

A small chapel in England had a custom for their service at night where a candle was placed at the end of each pew. When the family that usually sat in that pew arrived, the candle was lit. If the family did not come to the service, the candle was not lit and the pew remained dark. The amount of light in the church was determined by the number of families present that evening.

I wonder sometimes whether we light candles for Christ by our presence or whether we continue to aid the darkness by our absences, disinterest, conflicts or struggles in the church fellowship. Paul admonishes us "to build up the body of Christ."

Acceptance of Others

If we are truly a united church, there will be love and acceptance of one another. We acknowledge that we all may have differences of opinions and philosophies about theology or church government, but we are called to be the body of Christ, to work as his servants, and seek to do God's will in our lives and in the world. Therefore, we accept each other, because we have been accepted by Christ when we were sinners and forgiven of our sins.

In the Church of the Savior in Washington, D.C., a good example of acceptance was seen in the testimony of a woman named Meg. Her life had been ruined by alcohol. She had tried marriage, but continued to fall in the gutter as a prostitute. Her husband, who had been a war veteran, was so torn by depression at what had happened in their marriage that he had to be institutionalized for some time. But one day Meg's life was radically changed. She met Jesus Christ as Lord, and her life was completely changed. In that small church, she genuinely met Christ. She stopped drinking, quit swearing, gave up her life of prostitution, and her marriage was saved. She even went back to some of her old haunts and shared with those people the change that had been made in her life. She said that she came to this church and those people accepted her. They cared for her and gave themselves to her as no one had ever done before. "At first," she said, "I thought these people were crazy. Then I didn't care what they were. I suddenly wanted what they had."

Here is the real church. When the church really exhibits the fellowship of Christ, then people will want what we have. They don't want to be a part of any organization which is filled with divisiveness, fussing, and fighting. They want to be a part of a genuine fellowship where Christ is Lord and where people care for one another. Jesus said, "A new commandment I give unto you, 'Love one another'" (John 15:12). Writing in the small epistle of John, the writer declares: "That which was from the beginning, which we have heard, which we have seen with our own eyes; which we have looked upon and touched with our hands, concerning the word of life - the life was made manifest, and we saw it, and testify to it, and proclaim also to you the eternal life which is with the Father and was made manifest to us- it which we have seen and heard we proclaim also to you, so that you may have fellowship with us; our fellowship is with the Father and with his Son Jesus Christ" (I John 1:1-3).

Here then is the unique Christian fellowship. We enter this fellowship through a commitment of faith in Jesus Christ as Lord. We take upon ourselves the concern then of our fellow Christians and encourage one another by helping bear the burdens of one another and serving together as the united body of Christ. The greatness of our congregation will ultimately not be judged by the beauty of our sanctuary, the size of our staff, the education of our congregation, but by the way we love one another and serve Christ. Our fellowship will be real only as we model our lives after Christ. God grant that we will truly be the fellowship of Christ.

[1] Dietrich Bonhoeffer, *The Cost of Discipleship*, (London: SCM Press, 1959), 212

[2] Benjamin Garrison, *Portrait of the Church: Warts and All* (New York: Abingdon Press, 1964), 101.

[3] Carlyle Marney, *Priests To Each Other*, (Valley Forge, Judson   Press, 1974), 20.

[4] Morton Kelsey, *Discernment: A Study in Ecstasy and Evil*, (New York: Paulist Press, 1978), 83.

8.
THE REPUTATION OF A CHURCH
How to Behave in Church

It was pre-air-conditioned days, on a very hot summer day. The congregation sat behind their funeral fans which were kept constantly in motion as the preacher was "going at" his sermon. They were not too much into it, It was not simply because of the heat, but because he was so poorly prepared. They knew it, and he knew it. He was glad when it was "done," and so were they. The music was poorly prepared, poorly presented - nobody sang the hymns well and nobody really seemed to care. Everybody was glad when the service was over.

The preacher stood at the door as the people filed by. They made such incisive observations as, "Hot day, ain't it preacher?" "It's dry, we sure need rain." Then the preacher noticed a stranger coming through the line. He didn't like that unfamiliar face because for some reason it made him uneasy. Finally the stranger stood in front of the preacher, and the preacher extended his hand and said, "My name is Robin." The stranger said, "I know." "And your name?" "Oh, I'm just a watchman." "A watchman?" the preacher asked. "Yes, a watchman," the stranger replied. The preacher said, "Well, come back." And the watchman asked, "Why?" The preacher never forgot that question. It changed his whole ministry. He vowed to take worship leadership seriously.[1] We will have people of all kinds come in the doors of a particular church and meet you and me as members of that church. And you may ask them to come back, or you may ask them to come visit your church, and some of them may ask: "Why?" As people come to our church building, and as they see you and me in the world, the reputation of our church will be established, and our reputation will make all the difference whether or not people will be interested in the Church. Our reputation as a church will either attract or repel people.

How to Behave In Church

Paul gives us, in his Epistle to young Timothy (I Timothy 3:14-15), some guidance on how to behave in church. The words translated "behave" really mean conduct not only within an assembly like this but how one conducts his or her life and character in the world as well. But I think that Paul does still have in mind some sense of the Church gathered together as well as the way one conducts his life in the world, because Paul has just finished talking to young Timothy about the officers in the Church. We ought to learn from Paul how to "behave" in the Assembly of God.

Christians Care for One Another

People ought to sense that we really do care for each other. It was said of early Christians, "Behold how they loved one another." (1 John 4:7-12). When people come to a church, they ought to sense that it is really a warm, friendly, hospitable church where people care for one another. I heard recently about a personal study a man had made from visiting in worship services of various churches. He had a certain number that he would give a church if anybody spoke to him, before or after the service, or if somebody asked him if he were a visitor, or they shook hands with him, or they invited him back, etc. After the service was over, he` would walk all the way down to the front of the church and then go down the other aisle to see if he could initiate some kind of contacts in a church. Some churches never even got a "one", and the highest any church could get was a "ten." Rarely did a church get to a "five."

I know something about the experience of going into a church service where I was a total stranger to the people and discovering that often not a single soul ever said, "Welcome." "Come back again." "It's, good to have had you." That is a bad kind of reputation for a church to have.

When Arthur John Gossip was a very young assistant preacher to the famous Alexander Whyte, Dr. Whyte noticed that he was not in service the previous. Sunday, and he asked the young preacher where he was. Gossip said, "I was supplying in such and such church." Whyte asked him, "How did you find it?" He said, "Cold." Dr. Whyte said: "I preached there two years ago, and I have not been able to get the chill out of my bones since." It would be tragic indeed if people came into a church service and they experienced from others such a coldness in attitude that we communicate to them that we really do not care whether they are present or not. It is an unfortunate message for a church to declare one way or another. I trust they will see that we really want to be their friends. Friends share in each other's lives.

Friends are not concerned simply with how to use each other, but how they can support and encourage one another. I hope people will be friendly in their churches so that when a stranger comes in your church you will take the time to get to know them, introduce them to others, and let them feel a sense of welcome there. I hope our churches will have a reputation of being open-armed to new-comers. Let us say to them: "We are glad that you have come here, and we welcome you into the household of God."

Concerned About the Needs of Others

I hope we will also learn how to behave in church so that people will see that we are really concerned about the needs of other people (Galatians 6:2). I want people to speak of the church as one that cares when people are hurting, lonely and in distress. Years ago in Korea a native knocked on the door of a church and asked: "Is this the place where you mend broken hearts?" They should have said "yes."

The Church is the place where we mend broken hearts, broken relationships, and broken bodies. Here is the place where we reach out to all who feel that they are in pieces. We offer redemption through Jesus Christ, who gives wholeness, fullness, and togetherness. I hope that churches will not be exclusive clubs of a few, but a fellowship which reaches out to our society, to all those who are hurting, lonely, and aching. May we reach out to the young, couples, the elderly, the students in high school and those in college. Let's reach out to those in middle age, those who are rich or poor, and those who are needy or prestigious. We shall say to them through our programs, our teachings, and our worship, that we want to enable them to find their needs met by the power and presence of Jesus Christ. I hope that we shall develop that kind of reputation.

A number of years ago when the weather was very cold, a prosperous business man came out of his office, walked into the street and pulled his overcoat up around his neck and pulled his hat down tightly on his head as the gusty, freezing wind blew into his face. He saw a small boy leaning up against a building nearby. He walked over and said, "Son, you shouldn't be here. You will freeze. You need to get in out of this cold." The young lad began to explain why he was there. He had lost a five dollar bill which his father had given him to go buy some groceries. The man said, "Well, son, simply go home and tell your father what has happened." The boy said, "1 can't do that. My daddy is drinking now, and when he drinks he is in a violent mood. He will never understand. He will simply beat me."

The man did what should have been done. He took the small boy to the grocery store, bought him his groceries and gave him what change he had left from the five dollar bill so that he could take it home. As the young boy was getting ready to pick up his groceries, he turned around, came up and hugged the man, and said: "Mister, I *wish* you was my daddy."

Now there are a lot of people in our world who have lost more than a five dollar bill. Some of them have lost jobs, some of them have lost family relationships, and some of them have lost loved ones by death. There are people everywhere who have needs of all kinds to which you and I should respond. We need too be a spiritual father or mother or brother or sister to them. May we learn to be church for them. I hope we will conduct ourselves so that people will see us as friendly, caring people.

What Is Our Name?

A church gets its reputation by its name. Churches receive their names for all kinds of reasons. Some churches get their names because of their geography. They are Fifth Avenue Presbyterian Church, River Road Baptist Church, or Madison Avenue Baptist Church. Some churches get their names because of chronology. They are First Baptist Church, or Second Baptist Church. Some of them get their names from Christian virtues. They are Grace Methodist Church, Good Hope Baptist Church, or New Hope Presbyterian Church. Some get their names from doctrines like Calvary Baptist Church, The Church of the Redeemer, and the Lutheran Church of the Trinity. Some get their names from names like St. James, or Smith Memorial Pentecostal Church, Some get their names from biblical figures like Antioch Baptist

Church, Jerusalem Baptist Church, or Palestine Baptist Church.

In his letter Paul taught Timothy about the name a church really should have. The name of the church should be the Church of the Living God (I Timothy 3: 15). It is a church in which the living, vital presence of God is seen and experienced.

The Name of the Living God

A church's real strength is not just in numbers. Our strength is not in the size of our institutional church, but our strength is in the living God. It is the Lord upon whom we depend and upon whom the foundation of the church is built (1 Cor. 3:11). We have been entrusted to share the truth about this living God with other people. And so the early Christians gathered together in the name of the Living God. This was contrasted, as Paul was telling Timothy, with the God in the Temple at Ephesus who was cold and dead. Our Lord is a living God. In contrast with the gods in the Temple of Diana, which have been made with human hands, the Christian worships a "Living God." We gather to worship to attune our ears to God's voice; attune our eyes to God's presence; and to attune our lives to God's guidance. We gather to worship God, to hear something about God's presence among us, to see something of the trail of God's garment among us; and to seek God's guidance for all of our living.

Prepare For Worship

We gather that we might acknowledge the living God of the universe. This means that we do not come carelessly into God's presence. We come into the presence of the eternal God of the universe. Our worship is an acknowledgement that in the sacred place where we gather, we shall prepare to meet God. We know this meeting is mysterious, therefore we are coming to prepare ourselves by pausing, and hopefully praying, that we might sense God's presence among us.

During the time of the quiet prelude at the beginning of the service, our conversation and friendliness should begin to cease so that we might prepare ourselves to worship the living God of the universe. Having met God in worship, we shall pause a moment after the benediction for a time of silence. Then after praying silently, we lift our voices in praise to God in the doxology as we go forth to serve God in the world. Let the reputation of our churches focus on a church that gathers to worship in the name of the Living God.

A Pillar of Truth

Paul *says as* we gather in the name of the living God we shall be a church in which there is "a pillar and bulwark of truth" (1 Timothy 3: 15). Ephesus knew a great deal about pillars. The temple of Diana, which was located there, was surrounded by 127 pillars, most of them made of marble. Some of them were inlaid with jewels. Others were overlaid in gold. Each column was given by some lauded king. This temple, with its 127 pillars, was considered one of the Seven Wonders of the World.

In this epistle, Paul told the Church that all Christians are to be its pillars. We are to be that pillar-like element where people can see the truth radiating from our lives. We are to be the bulwark or the support which keeps the building square and intact. The Church (its members) has been entrusted with sharing the truth about Jesus Christ with the world. The Gospel truth and story is neither your private secret nor mine. We are entrusted to share the good news of *Jesus Christ* with all persons. It is the good news of the God who has become incarnate and lived among us and taught us how to live. God has come through Christ and died for us, was raised, and has come now in the Spirit to instill the Church with the power of his presence. We have been entrusted to share that truth with the world. Without the ministry of the Church, the message of the Gospel might go un-preserved and un-proclaimed.

A Teaching and Preaching Church

This means we must be a teaching and preaching church (1Timothy 6:3-4). Having received this great gift of God, we go now to our people and teach them to observe all that Christ has demanded us. We teach the truth from the Scriptures so men and women will know more about God and how to live in God's way. We are entrusted to keep the truth sane and understandable so people can respond to it. In a day when there is so much pseudo-religion, and Christianity has been identified with the American way of life, and we have a caricature of religion and too much distorted and twisted religion, we need to dig deeper into the Scriptures to try to understand what it means to be the living church of Christ in the world today.

As we call people to follow the Christ-like way, we should not be embarrassed or ashamed to tell them that it is costly. The Christian way costs one a commitment in life to Christ and a radical change in one's life. We do not compromise it for individuals by saying: "Well, it doesn't make any difference what you believe - just come on - we need you." Jesus did not compromise his message so that the rich young ruler would follow him, but he lifted up for him the same demands of the gospel and said, "Come, follow me." Unashamedly, we say Jesus Christ seeks to draw all persons to him, but we acknowledge at the same time, that it is not a cheap grace. It has cost God his life through his Son, and it has caused his atoning death.

We are invited now to walk in that kind of sacrificial way. We are the pillar and bulwark of truth. The truth is not within us, but we are entrusted to share this great truth with others so they, too, can find the power of the living Christ. We trust the power of the Gospel to do its work.

A man once came back home to a small country church. He had not been there in a number of years for worship and noticed a man who was sitting up in front of the church and he was startled by his presence. He remembered that man from his boyhood days as the noted atheist in the community. He drank so much his family was impoverished. Once he blasphemed and literally dared God to strike him dead with lightning. Small children were afraid even to walk near him because they thought that God might open up the earth and swallow him and all those nearby. It was hard to believe that this man was sitting in church with his whole family. They filled up a ten-foot pew. He learned later that this man had been converted and his life changed. He noticed, as the preacher finished his sermon that day, that there was a tear on the man's cheek. No nodding came from this man, because he knew the radical change that Jesus Christ could bring to life. Seeing the change in that man's life, he said: "I must commit more of my time to an institution like the church which has done so much to change somebody like that man." The church has been challenged to reach out with the truth to change individuals to be more like the Christ with his redeeming wholeness. It is a message that all need to hear.

A Singing Church

Notice also that Paul says to Timothy that the Church was a singing Church. He concludes this section by reaching back and giving us what was probably a part of an early confessional hymn (1 Timothy 3: 16). The Church from its beginning was a singing church (Ephesians 5: 19, Colossians 3: 16-17). Music was a part of its life. The Church drew from the synagogue hymns which they had read from the Old Testament like the 100th Psalm, "Make a joyful noise to the Lord, all the lands! Serve the

Lord with gladness! Come into his presence with singing!"

The Church has always been a singing church. The Church patterned its service after the worship it was used to in the synagogue. Even Jesus at his last supper probably sang one of the Passover psalms. The Bible and the hymnbook have gone down through the years as a part of the life of the church. The hymn book has been for many their devotional guide in understanding God, themselves, and life. The hymn book somehow has been able to convey something about the mystery of religion for common people through the ages. Music is something that the Church shares together which bridges all denominational lines.

I hope, by the variety and quality of our music, that people who come will sense something moving and theologically powerful in the words which are proclaimed through song. Now I am no great singer, but I have always liked singing. When our church services were broadcast on the radio, I was always advised to stand back a little from the microphone while we are singing. I think they told me that for several reasons. But nevertheless I have sung in choirs, and have enjoyed singing! There is something lacking in our lives when we simply pick up the hymn book, or we do not even open it, or we just stand there. Learn to mouth the words if you can't sing. Share in the music in some way. Let our reputation as a singing church go forth.

Several years ago my family and I had the privilege of going back to the church where I had been pastor in Bristol, Virginia for the celebration of the 25th anniversary of their church choir tours, These tours have been led for 25 consecutive years by Joann Feazell, who served as Minister of Music in that church for forty years. They had a banquet on Saturday night in which young people and adults gave testimony about what this music ministry had meant in their lives. The next day, on Sunday morning, the whole center section of the church was filled with people who had come back for this special celebration. Some of them came from as far away as Florida for this occasion. In that center section there were doctors, bankers, ministers, ministers of music, student directors, and persons of all ages from youth to middle age. Their mature voices made their anthems sound glorious. Nobody will ever convince me that the power of music cannot have a powerful effect upon the lives of persons.

In a singing church, our lives can be transformed. I appreciate what our adult choir does, and I hope their music will be meaningful and their faithfulness will be constant. Music is such a vital part of the medium through which young people express themselves that we need to make it available in a strong way in our church. I hope our children's choirs, and all of the other ways we share in musically will give some picture of this church's reputation about the importance we give to singing praises unto God. I hope we can learn to do it well. Those of us who may not be good musicians can do like our silent friends who are deaf and without speech, we can "sign" our praise or silently lift our inner voice in praise to God. Each week through our singing we testify and bear witness to something of this truth about Christ. I trust the church will always have a reputation of being a singing church.

The Mystery of Religion

Paul speaks here about the deep mysteries of our religion. The mystery which Paul was talking about is a mystery which was once hidden but has now been made known. This mystery nobody could comprehend and understand. The Church could see that the mystery religions surrounding them wanted to keep their religion secret and hidden in their temples. The Christian Church declared a mystery about God's nature and his love which has been made clear for us.

If there are individuals who want to draw you into some kind of secret, mystical, mysterious cult, and say that they have more religious insight, understand they are going in opposition to the New Testament faith. The mystery which Paul was speaking about was a mystery revealed. This mystery disclosed the nature of God and was not delivered for a special few but was for all persons, so we could understand what this great God is like.

Look at the parallelism that Paul made here. He compared spirit and flesh, angels and nations, the world as people knew it and the glory to follow. He wrote about Christ who was manifested in the flesh as the incarnation of God. Flesh itself was not seen as evil. God himself became flesh and dwelt among us. He was "manifested in the flesh" which meant that his humanity was real. He speaks here also about the one who "has been vindicated by the spirit." It was God's spirit that raised him from the dead demonstrating that he was not a false Messiah but the real one.

The statement that "he has been seen by angels" may be a reference to Christ's pre-existence, or certainly it is a reference that Christ is more powerful than angels. Angels themselves give witness and testimony to whom and what Christ is. "That he has been proclaimed among all nations" is a reference not just for the Jewish selected few, but that he is preached for all people. "He is believed," Paul says, "by all peoples." This expansion of the good news of Christ is carried to all persons, and he is glorified in heaven in his ascension when he was "taken up into glory." In this one great portion of a hymn, Paul tells us some glorious truths about Christ.

A Final Summons

Let the reputation of this church go forth that we are a church which cares for each other. We are a people assembled together in friendship and concern to meet each other's needs. I hope that people will sense that the name of the church, whatever it is, represents a place where the living God dwells among us to guide us into all kinds of ministries both new and old. May our reputation be one of a church that is a bulwark and pillar of truth. May others know that we are unafraid to face any questions or issues, and that we are open and struggling to understand what the presence of God among us means. May the reputation of the church reveal to others the joy of Christ which fills our lives with meaning.

Years ago, before they had the more sophisticated ways of communication, and they had to use drum beats to indicate how an army was to proceed, a captain came up to his drummer and said, "Sound the retreat." The drummer said, "Captain, I don't know a retreat. But I can beat a charge." He could beat a charge, and he did. And they went forward and won the battle. I hope you will not want to retreat into some private corner and be something else other than what God wants you to be. I hope we, as a church, will charge forth to be his people and do his will and his work in the world. It is time to move forward in faith and hope and not to retreat in despair and hopelessness.

[1] J. Wallace Hamilton, *Where Now Is Your God?* (Old Tappan, New Jersey: Fleming H. Revell Co., 1969), 91-92.

9.
Will It Really Make Much Difference?
The Church as the Salt of the Earth

When I was a boy, one Sunday afternoon my family was helping prepare the meal for a family reunion. My younger brother and I had been charged with freezing the homemade ice cream. We got out our White Mountain hand-crank freezer, gathered up the ice and rock salt and started our job. We took turns turning the crank on the freezer for what seemed like hours to us. But I'm sure it wasn't. But for two small boys it did seem like a long time indeed. We finally checked the ice cream and it seemed hard to us. Later the real test of the ice cream came—the eating. You know what had happened. You may have had this problem yourself, if you have ever made homemade ice cream. There was no way we could disguise, hide or ignore what had happened. The ice cream was salty. And salty ice cream just isn't very good. We had let the salt get into the cream and its presence spoke for itself. It could not be disguised. Its appearance was evident to all.

Jesus said to his disciples, "You are to be salt to the world" (Matthew 5: 13). This saying is a part of what is usually called the Sermon on the Mount. This sermon was addressed primarily to Jesus' disciples. There may have been others in a crowd nearby who overheard it, but the Sermon on the Mount was addressed to the disciples of Jesus. The first part in this sermon focuses on the inner person or the characteristics of what it means to be a disciple-- those persons who are a part of the Kingdom of God. The emphasis was not on what you do but on who you are as a child of God. In this section the characteristics of the kingdom disciple are humility, grief over one's sins, gentleness, righteousness, a merciful nature, purity of thought, waging peace, and the willingness to suffer in the cause of righteousness.

You Will Penetrate the World

Following the beatitude declaration, there is a shift in the emphasis from the inner person to the external life. Now a new direction is asserted. If a disciple has these inner characteristics, how will he or she live? The focus falls now on their action. The religion of the heart needs to find expression in daily living. What is within a person must be expressed outwardly. The idea must take on form and shape in one's life. What will be the effect that the disciples will have on the world because they have been changed internally? As a disciple, you are to be salt. The Church will make a difference only if is "the salt of the earth."

Valuable as Salt

In the ancient world, salt had much more value than it seems to have in our society today. Salt is so common and ordinary today. In some parts of the ancient world, a bag of salt was considered more valuable than a man's life. In the Roman world, soldiers were often paid in salt. This practice became the root for the word salary. There is a statement in the Jewish Talmud that salt symbolizes the Torah. Just as the world cannot exist with salt, so the world cannot exist without the Torah. Homer had referred to salt as "divine." Jesus drew on these rich images about salt when he told his disciples; "You are to be salt to the world."

A Duty to Be Salty

I believe that this statement from Jesus comes first as a call to duty. Jesus didn't say, "You might be salt," or, "You should be salt," or, "You have salt." He said about his disciples, "You ARE salt." It is the duty of salt to be salty. This was not simply a compliment but recognition of their new character. This then was a commission, an announcement of the mission of the disciples and the Church. "This is what your influence or your impact is to be on the world. You are to be salt. The inner characteristics of my disciples as children of the Kingdom of God compel them to have an impact on the world as they penetrate the world with God's grace in their lives." Jesus said his disciples would be "salted with fire" (Mark 9:49).

An Impact

As salt, you will make an impact. If you have a cut and get salt in it, you know how that wound bites of stings from the contact with the salt. When Jesus comes into our lives, sometimes there is a biting or stinging influence because of our hurts, wounds or sins. Often there is no healing without some pain. In Bernanos' novel entitled, *The Diary of a Country Priest*, the writer observes that Jesus did not say, "You are the honey of the world," but instead, "You are the salt of the earth." The disciples of Jesus are to be the force that makes such an impact in society that sometimes its impact might be stinging and biting.

A Summons to Duty

Salt also has a characteristic of making us thirsty. The disciples, who have been commissioned to be salty, should create a sense of thirst for persons in the world for God. If we create that kind of thirst, Jesus stands ready to be the one to quench that thirst and lead all persons to God. "If anyone thirst, let them come unto me and drink" (John 7:37). This may be the first emphasis of this saying. As disciples, you are the salt of the earth with a commission—a call to duty and responsibility to be salty.

An Inconspicuous Difference

Secondly, would you not agree with me that Jesus may be using a figure in the image of salt which indicates the gradual, quiet and inconspicuous way the kingdom has its effect in the world? When salt is put in food, you really don't want to notice the salt when you eat the food. You just want to notice the difference that it makes in the taste of the food. If there is too much salt in the food, it will ruin the taste just like it did in the freezer of ice cream I made when I was a boy. But if salt is doing its proper, important work, it is inconspicuous. Sometimes the disciples of Jesus are inconspicuous in the world, and at other times they may be light. Jesus also told his disciples, "You are the light of the world." At other times a disciple may be brilliant or flashing like a light. You may be visible. But I am convinced that most often the best work for Christ is done quietly, gently, and inconspicuously in the world.

Bigness as a Measure of Success

But the emphasis in our age for measuring success is often on bigness- the size of one's bank account, stocks and bonds or the size and number of houses one owns. Years ago P. T. Barnum advertised an elephant he had in his circus named Jumbo as the largest animal in captivity. Someone has suggested that this might be a good image for our age --"the age of Jumboism." Can the real value or worth of much in our society be measured by its size or quantity? Remember that the world's largest animal became extinct, and the world's largest bird can't even fly. When the ostrich sees danger threatening it, it sticks its head in the sand to hide. It thinks it is safe. I have often wondered if the church doesn't stick its head in the sand like the ostrich at times and is unwilling to face some of its real problems and makes the mistake of measuring its worth by the size of its numbers or financial worth.

Overlooking the Inconspicuous

The importance of the minute is obscured by this pseudo emphasis on bigness. Some of the most powerful forces in the world are small and inconspicuous. I think of the power of the microscopic atom. The lowly earthworm ever so gradually and quietly does its work in decomposition of soil. Bacteria carry out their duty inconspicuously. Who sees their work without a microscope? If the seeds of our food source failed to reproduce, what would we do for food? The optic nerve in your eye is small and insignificant in size, yet if it is damaged, we cannot see. Who thinks about the tiny nerves in a tooth until suddenly we have a toothache? Look at the revolution created by the microchip and computer chip. Look at the difference they have made in revolutionizing the world. These products or forces are all seemingly small and inconspicuous but what a radical difference they make in our world.

Jesus told his disciples, "You, you, YOU are the salt." Who in the world would have thought that this group of fishermen, tax collectors and uneducated persons—a motley crew at best—could be the force to change society? Yet Jesus seemed to be saying, "You will be that very instrument." The remarkable thing was that they did indeed become such a force to transform the world.

The Power of God in Our Hand

How different God's standard often is from ours. We do not realize the power God has placed in your hand and mine to serve God. We are called to be a part of Jesus' disciples who will make a radical difference in society. Do you remember when Moses received his commission from God that he had a shepherd's staff in his hand? God asked him, "What is that in your hand?" Moses replied, "A shepherd's staff." God said, "Throw it down on the ground." When Moses did, the staff was transformed into a snake. When he took his staff before Pharaoh, it became an instrument to reveal the power of God. "What is in your hand, Moses?" Power that comes from God.

"What is in your hand, young David?" He had only a few stones as he stood before the giant Goliath. Yet those stones became evidence of the power of God. "What is that in your hand, Samson?" It's only the jawbone of a jackass. What is that before such a crowd of enemies? It is insignificant. But with the power of God, he was victorious over his enemies. "What is that in your hand, Jesus?" It's only a few pieces of bread and some fish, but you need to feed a multitude. When blessed by God, five thousand persons were fed. Think what is in your hand and mine to serve God in the world. We are to be salt to transform society.

This small group of disciples seemed to have such an unlikely possibility of making any real difference in the world of the first century. Yet, this small band of believers, gathering in homes in Jerusalem, Thessalonica, Ephesus, Corinth, Rome or in the house of a woman named Lydia, who was the seller of purple in Philippi, and in other places, became the spark that ignited the fire of Christ that would sweep around the world. Fishermen, tax collectors, slaves, and other men and women became the salt that gave the church its start. Like leaven and a grain of mustard seed, the church was launched by a small fellowship of believers. God often works inconspicuously through ordinary men and women in a variety of places.

A Symbol for Purity

Go another step further with me and note that salt in the ancient world was sometimes a symbol for purity. Salt was used to administer cleansing. Jesus may have been saying to his disciples, "You are to be the purifying force in the world." In the beatitudes, Jesus had declared that, "The pure in heart shall see God" (Matt. 5:8). You are to be those "holy" persons in society who can make a radical difference for good. Paul reminds us "to present our bodies as a holy sacrifice unto God" (Rom. 12:1). "Be holy in all conversation," wrote Peter (I Peter 1:15). We are to live righteous lives like our Lord. Others will know by our living that we are the disciples of Jesus. If people cannot see any difference in your life and mine and that of non-Christians in the world, then the answer must clearly be that we are not truly a Christian disciple. Jesus said, "You will know them by their fruits" (Matt. 7:16). The disciples of Jesus will be known by their salty quality in the world.

Several years ago when another church I served as pastor was looking for an assistant minister, I received the following letter of reference from one of the young man's former college professors. "There is something wonderfully clean about the young man, and the reference there is to his mind as well as to his physical being. He is unfailingly a gentleman . . . He is loyal to the very highest ideals, and he has both the intelligence and the character to render estimable service to those ideals. I believe that if there is one word that summarizes his many splendid qualities, it is integrity, and I like to think of the relationship of that word to an integer. He is a 'whole number,' solid and sound and unblemished." Obviously, we called him. What a marvelous reference.

We exemplify our Christian commitment by the moral lives we live. True disciples of Christ will reflect in their lives Christ-like characteristics.

A Seasoning or Flavoring Ingredient

Then go another step and notice that salt is also used to give seasoning or flavor to our food. In Job we read, "Can there be any taste in food if it is not salty?" (Job 6:6) Some translations read, "Can there be any taste in the white of an egg?" We know how bland the white of an egg can be. Christians should be the force in society that influences it for good. Christians should give a seasoning of encouragement, zest, peace, trust, love and worship. Christians are the righteous element overcoming the negative spirit of discouragement, disharmony, and disunity. Salty Christians work for the unity of the body of Christ. As salt, they seek to overcome the flat, tasteless, insipid quality of life and should permeate the world with a real joy and zest for life. Rather than being negative, they bring a pleasant, joyful, radiant, satisfying note into living.

The Joy of the Christian

C. S. Lewis entitled his autobiography, *Surprised by Joy*. Before he became a Christian, Lewis had always thought that Christianity was dull and boring, but when he became a Christian, he was surprised to find the joyous nature of the Christian life. Christians should provide that flavor to society and lift living to a higher plain.

When we were on vacation several years ago, we got up early one morning and decided to drive awhile before we ate breakfast. As we drove along on the road in North Dakota, we saw many signs advertising a place called "Walls Drug Store." Well, I'll be honest with you. I had never heard of Walls Drug Store. The further we drove into North Dakota, we began to see more and more signs which noted the many features of this store. The signs indicated that this place was far more than a drug store. They did have a restaurant, we noticed, and we needed to eat breakfast. Their advertisements attested to a wide variety of shops, stores, restaurants and places of amusements. All of these signs made us curious to see what this "drug store" was really like. We kept seeing the signs that read, "Free ice water." "Coffee, Five Cents a Cup." "Coffee, a nickel?" I thought. "Could that still be possible?" Soon we pulled off the expressway and drove into a small town and saw this huge enterprise called Walls Drug Store.

Walls Drug Store began back in the depression when a young druggist moved there with his wife. Their drug store struggled, and they wondered what they could do to attract more people to the drug store. As people drove along those roads on hot days without air conditioning, they soon got thirsty. One day they decided that the one thing they could offer people was cool water. They began with a simple advertisement: "Free Ice Water." People began to drive off the road to get their free ice water. While drinking their water, these people bought other things in the drug store. Slowly business improved and amazingly Walls Drug Store grew every year until its expansion became a worldwide phenomenon. Write-ups about this drugstore have appeared in *Life, Wall Street Journal, the New York Times, Time* magazine and in other American and European papers. This drug store had received an international reputation. What an influence from such a small beginning. By the way, the coffee was only five cents, there was free ice water, and the food was delicious. They indeed lived up to their reputation.

Should not the Christian "advertise" their "good news" and invite others to taste the joy they have known in Christ? Let them taste and see the joyful life of the Christian.

The Preservative Factor

However, I think that the basic thing that Jesus was saying about the disciples as salt denotes that the Christian should be the preservative force in society. Christians should be the element that preserves the world from decay. The disciples knew immediately what Jesus was talking about when he referred to salt. The fishermen among the disciples knew that as soon as they caught their fish, they had to salt them if they were going to keep them until they could get them to market. There was no refrigeration in that day. Without refrigeration, it was necessary to salt meat to preserve it. If you grew up on a farm years ago, many of you likely had no refrigeration and you know something about salting meat to preserve it. You may have salted hams and stored them.

I remember one time in Virginia inviting a friend from Louisiana to eat some country ham. He was not used to eating ham that had been salted and didn't like it very much. Salting meat is an ancient way of preservation.

Jesus is saying to his disciples, "You are to be like salt in society, to preserve it from corruption." You are to be that force in society that seeks to overcome its greed, lust, and selfishness. The Roman empire, in which Christianity had been born, did collapse. Christianity has survived decay all around it, through the Dark Ages to the Space Age. Christians are to be the salt that makes a real difference in the world.

The Christian Has to Live in the World

Christians cannot preserve society by living apart from the world, no more than salt can preserve meat if it stays in the salt shaker or box. Salt has to be put on food to make a difference. If you and I are going to make a difference in the world, we must come in contact with the world. Just as Jesus reached out and touched those in need, like the leper, the hurting, blind, deaf, poor, weak or sinful persons, so you and I need to be that force that reaches out and touches people with the power of God's grace. They need to see that Christ makes a difference in the way we live and think.

If our religion is genuine, it cannot be kept to ourselves. Throughout history, individuals have made a difference, because they have been willing to stand up for Christ. Those who have had a real impact did not try to keep their religion a secret. They made it known so others could know about Christ. Look at the list whose influence is still felt. Among them are Abraham, Moses, Ruth, Esther, Peter, John, Paul, Augustine, Lottie Moon, Helen Keller, Mother Teresa, and countless others. These persons have been salt in the world for God.

Christians are to be salt to the world. They are not to be salt merely inside a church building and not be concerned about the world. You are to be salt in your work. You are to be salt in your play, in your home wherever you are. Sometimes maybe you can be salt in the church. A minister went to a church one time that was divided by factions. One of the men in the church said, "The devil has the church." But an older man, who had been a member of that church a long time, remarked: "He hasn't got my seat yet. I am in it myself every service, and I am going to see to it that he does not get it." That man became a focal place in that church through whom God worked to turn it around. He chose to be salt.

Can Salt Lose Its Saltiness?

But Jesus reminds us that if salt loses its salty nature, it is good for nothing but to be trodden under the feet of people. We ask the question, "Can salt 1ose its salty characteristic?" Isn't salt always chloride of sodium? Chemically, can salt be anything other than it is? As long as there is any particle of it left, is it not still salt? There are some scholars who say that statement indicates the impossibility of a real disciple being anything other than salt. You have to be salt if you are a follower of Christ.

In the first century, however, pure salt did not exist. Salt was often mixed with a residue along the Dead Sea, or other places they gathered it. Sometimes real salt would be washed out of the composite and only the residue would remain. What was that residue good for? It was good for nothing. There was no salty quality remaining. It was without value. Jesus was saying that his disciples are to be salt, and if we don't exhibit that salty characteristic, then we are really good for nothing. Salt that has lost its savor was only to be thrown on the street to be trodden under foot. In one of the other gospels, it read that saltless salt should be "thrown on the dung hill."

Christians without salt are absolutely without any value, because they are supposed to be salty in their service for Christ. If Christians lose their distinctive quality and become like the world, they are worthless.

Joy in Christ

What does it mean today for us not to be salty as Christians? Well, for one thing, it means that these persons have lost their sense of joy in Christ. Joy has slipped out of their grasp. These persons are like a hot coal that has been removed from all the rest of the coals. In its isolation, it grows cold. When we are isolated from Christ, we grow cold. These persons have no sense of joy in serving Christ or living for him.

Indifference

A second sign is indifference. Indifferent persons have lost their thrill in following Christ and there is no desire to share Christ with others. The Book of Revelation describes the church at Laodicea as insipid. "I wish you were cold or hot. Since you are lukewarm and neither hot nor cold, I will spew you out of my mouth" (Rev. 3:15). When we become indifferent to the cause of Christ, we become worthless to him. Some have begun their pilgrimage with Christ, and then have fallen away. Others have placed their hand to the plow, but they have looked back. Others have buried their talent in the ground, or they have not counted the cost as they started to build a tower, or they have not continued until the end, as Jesus spoke about in several parables. All of these persons have started, but they could not continue. These persons fell away from Christ; therefore, they are worthless.

Religious Self-Satisfaction

There is another sign of salt without savor and that is being satisfied with religious delusion. These persons are willing to settle for a distorted image of the Christian. They accept the residue as salt. They are surrounded with the outward appearances of religion, but there is nothing within that is a genuine characteristic of Christ. We may have large buildings and huge budgets. We may have all kinds of programs and large numbers attending. But are these really the characteristics of what Christ wants his disciples to be in the world? We are called to be on mission for him. We are to change society. The church may be a nice social club or outstanding civic organization, or informative little study groups. But are we really salt? Are we a revolutionary force that is changing society? Are we really genuinely leading people to Christ, or do we just gather together and perpetuate ourselves and the institution we have built? Jesus Christ makes a demand on our life which is radical and calls us to be different in the way we live in the world. Sometimes our churches are merely a reflection of the world and not a reflection of Christ at all.

There is a story about Thomas Aquinas and the pope as they watched the crowd of faithful who came to the Jubilee bringing their bags of money for offerings. The pope leaned over to Aquinas, as the people passed, and said: "Peter could not say now, 'Silver and gold have I none.'" "No," Aquinas replied, "And neither could he say any longer, 'Arise, take up your bed and walk'"!

When the church becomes so identified with the world and its culture, it is no longer salt. It has become good for nothing! We need to ask ourselves individually and as a church, "Are we salt or are we good for nothing?" We might want to say that the church cannot lose its "savor," but often it has. Ask yourself, "Where are the churches of Asia Minor? Where are the churches of Alexandria, Antioch, and Constantinople? Where are the churches of North Africa where Augustine worshiped? They have been "trodden under the feet of those who passed by." In a Moslem mosque in Damascus, there is an inscription which is partially obliterated, "Thy Kingdom, O Christ, is an everlasting Kingdom," and inscribed over them are the words, "There is no God but God and Mohammed is his prophet."

Our institutional churches sometimes are transformed into something radically other than what our Lord intended for them to be. If the Church is going to make a difference in the world, it has to be the "salt of the earth." Christians are called to be salt to the world. Our model is Christ.

The Danger of Becoming Identified with the World

The subtle danger for the church is to be corrupted by and conformed to the world's image instead of being salt to the world, and transforming the world into Christ's likeness. We have been called not to conform to the world but to be transforming force in society by the power of the living Christ, who has transformed us. To be very honest with you, there are times I get very discouraged with the church. I have those feelings because I think we are so far from being what Christ really wants his church to be. We bring into our church the same pettiness that is in the world, the same self-seeking and power struggles. We bring the sins of the world into the church and refuse to let Christ transform us, forgive us and redirect us. How can we ever change the world and be salt when we haven't first been changed?

When I become discouraged like this, I remember a story I read about a painting which hung in one of our nation's galleries depicting Satan and Faust engaged in a chess match. Underneath the painting were written these words, "Checkmate." If you know anything about chess, you know that the word "checkmate" means the game is over. The king can make only limited moves, while the queen is the most versatile player on the board. Other pieces on the board have limited moves. One day a world champion chess player came into the art gallery and studied the painting for a long time, and then he exclaimed so that everybody in the gallery could hear him: "It's a lie. Both the king and the knight can move!"

There are times when people want to say that about the church. It has been checkmated. The knights – you and I, God's servants – can't move. It is over. But you remember. That is a lie. God can move! And we can move! We can be salt, the preserving force in the world. God is still working through his church to transform the world. God grant that you and I will let God use us as a salt. n

About the Author

Dr. William Powell Tuck, a native of Virginia, has been a pastor in Virginia, Kentucky, Louisiana, and North Carolina. He has also been a seminary professor and has taught adjunctively at several colleges and at the Baptist Theological Seminary at Richmond. He is the author of eighteen books, including *Our Baptist Tradition, The Ten Commandments: Their Meaning Today, The Compelling Faces of Jesus,* and *Love as a Way of Living.* He received the Parish Pastor of the Year award from the Academy of Parish Clergy in 1997 and an honorary Doctor of Divinity degree from the University of Richmond. He is married to Emily Campbell and is the father of two children and four grandchildren. He resides in Midlothian, Virginia. For more information about Dr. Tuck you may go to his website www.friarsfragment.com.